WALTER BLOCK

Defending the Undefendable II:
Freedom in All Realms

WALTER BLOCK

Defending the Undefendable II: Freedom in All Realms

Cartoon Illustrator: Charles Rodrigues

TERRA LIBERTAS

This edition first published in UK and USA 2013
by Terra Libertas Publishing House
Chantry House, 22 Upperton Road,
Eastbourne, East Sussex, BN21 1BF
United Kingdom
www.terralibertas.com

ISBN: 978-1-908089-37-3 (hardcover edition)

Contents

DEDICATION

T his book is dedicated to those who have been most influential in my recent thinking about issues of political economy: William Barnett, Lipa Dubrawsky, Michael Edelstein, Stephan Kinsella, and Hans Hoppe. I am indebted to Jeff Riggenbach for a splendid editorial job on this book; to Lew Rockwell for founding and running the Mises Institute, a source of inspiration for me over the years; to my colleagues at Loyola University New Orleans, particularly Bill Barnett, but also Dan D'Amico, John Levendis, Leo Krasnozhon, Nick Capaldi, and Stuart Wood, who have made the last several years of my academic life such a pleasure. I also dedicate this book to my literary agent, Mei Yao. She pushes me, leads me, inspires me, but always with a very delicate hand. This book would not have been published by Terra Libertas Publishing House without her help; nor without the important efforts of my publisher, Iulian Tănase. The following Loyola University New Orleans students were helpful in research, putting together this manuscript, doing the odds and sods necessary for the completion of such a project. They are: Andrew Naquin and especially Michael O'Brien, to whom I owe for much work over and above the call of duty. I also thank the Fraser Institute of Canada for permission to rely upon work I did while employed there, 1979–1991.

I dedicate this book, also, to my children, Matthew and Hannah. May they and their generation do their utmost to promote liberty.

FOREWORD

It is a pleasure to introduce *Defending the Undefendable II: Freedom in All Realms,* the latest book by my friend, Dr. Walter Block. This book is a sequel to Dr. Block's seminal 1976 work *Defending the Undefendable.*

The original book caused quite a stir and I suspect that Dr. Block's follow-up will prove even more controversial—and influential. This book should find a larger audience than the original, since many more Americans (especially young Americans) are now interested in the ideas of liberty. Furthermore, Dr. Block was a young and relatively unknown scholar in 1976, whereas today he is widely recognized as one of the liberty movement's most important intellectuals.

As for controversy, how could a book which purports to defend corporate raiders, human-organ merchants, and polygamists not be controversial? I have no doubt that even many libertarians will at least initially react with shock and outrage at some portions of the book. Some may also wonder how a pro-life, Christian, culturally conservative libertarian like me can endorse this book.

I endorse Dr. Block's book for the same reason culturally conservative libertarians such as F. A. Hayek and Murray Rothbard endorsed the first in this series: despite the misleading title, Dr. Block's purpose is not to defend "indefensible" activities, but the worthy basis of libertarianism: the non-aggression axiom.

The non-aggression axiom is the simple idea that it is immoral to initiate force against another person or their property. This axiom follows logically from a belief in private property rights, including the individual's property interest in his or her own body. After all, if people have a right to control their own bodies and property, it cannot be moral to forcefully prevent them from engaging in activities which do not violate the rights of others—even if such activities are widely considered immoral.

Most people support applying the non-aggression axiom to private conduct. What distinguishes libertarians from modern conservatives and liberals is that we apply the non-aggression axiom to the government! To libertarians, *any* use of force to change people's behavior for any reason is a profoundly immoral act. Furthermore, state action to forbid or regulate individual behavior always has unintended consequences that often harm the very people the state claims will benefit from the intervention!

For example, minimum wage laws, by outlawing work below a state-set wage, shove those at the bottom of the income and experience ladder out of the job market. The drug war simply creates incentives for drug dealers to sell increasingly stronger and more dangerous drugs while discouraging drug addicts from seeking help. I saw an example of this in my years as an OB-GYN: patients who used illegal drugs were oftentimes reluctant to share with me their history of drug use for fear that it would result in their imprisonment. Obviously this made it more difficult for me to protect the health of the woman and her unborn child.

Adherence to the non-aggression axiom in no way implies approval of behaviors like drug use. Many, if not most, libertarians have strong moral objections to the behaviors like drug use and pornography. However libertarians recognize the only moral and effective way to combat these behaviors is through the peaceful means of education and moral persuasion. Private institutions such as strong families, communities, and churches are much more effective at instilling moral values than laws or government programs. Of course, libertarians also oppose any government attempt to force people to subsidize, associate with, or otherwise support lifestyle choices they find morally objectionable or self-destructive. A society where individuals bear the responsibility for their own actions would see much less drug abuse and other harmful behaviors than one in which the government effectively subsidizes the problems resulting from self-destructive behaviors.

Dr. Block also points out that consistent adherence to the non-aggression axiom will resolve many, if not most, areas of social conflicts. In a free society, property owners could decide whether or not to allow smoking on their property, and what constitutes a valid marriage. Respecting the rights of property and contracts would also provide for efficient environmental protection. In a libertarian society, for example, oil companies would have incentives to drill for oil in the most efficient and safe manner possible because they would be liable for all harm caused by their actions.

The non-aggression axiom is thus not an invitation to libertinism; it is instead rooted in the recognition of one of the natural rights of all humans to life, liberty, and property. If there is one area where I disagree with Walter Block, it is that I wish he spent more time separating libertarianism from libertinism.

However, that in no way diminishes the value of this new work, which will hopefully serve, as Roger Lea MacBride said of the original book, as "Drano for clogged minds." I am confident that *Defending the Undefendable II: Freedom in All Realms* will show a new generation the importance of consistent adherence to the non-aggression axiom.

Ron Paul, U.S. Congress, 14th District, Texas

INTRODUCTION

In 1974, when I began putting together the collection of iconoclastic essays that eventually came to be known as *Defending the Undefendable* (1976 Fleet, 1991 Fox and Wilkes, 2008 Mises Institute, 2013 Terra Libertas), my purpose was simple and easily stated. It was to promote an appreciation of libertarianism by applying it to the "hard" cases.

What is libertarianism? This is the political philosophy that asks but one question, and gives but one answer. The question? When is force or the threat of force justified? The answer? Only in response to, or in defense from, or in retaliation against, the prior use of violence against a person or his legitimately owned property. And what is its source? How does virgin territory properly become converted into private property? Again libertarianism is succinct: through homesteading, and any subsequent legitimate form of title transfer. Homesteading consists of mixing your labor with the land or other unowned parts of nature, and property may be legitimately transferred from one person to another through any voluntary non-fraudulent means: sale, gift, barter, trade, gambling, inheritance, etc.

This mode of converting nature into appropriable property for mankind has been criticized when it comes to land most, appreciated precisely for its pristine virtues; for example, a stand of redwood trees or the Grand Canyon. But even here, there is *some* mixing of labor that can establish ownership:

clearing away dead branches, creating paths and building bathroom facilities, etc., so that the land may be more readily enjoyed. This is not a "perfect" solution to the problem, but all the alternatives are far worse. One possibility is to grant ownership to government. But there are two problems with that option. First, the minions of the state have done nothing to demonstrate ownership; they have not mixed *their* labor with this land. Secondly, government is itself an invasive institution, in that it forces people to join against their will, and will not allow them to leave (laws against secession). Another possibility is to convert virgin territory into private property through mere announcement. The difficulty, here, is that anyone can verbally claim anything he wants, and disputes will continue. I hereby claim the sun, the moon and the stars, and so do you. The rightful owner is still to be determined. A third possibility is to divide all property up equally, for everyone in the world. Thus, we would each own one six billionth of all territory on the planet. But this would be a recipe for non-action with regard to land, due to very long committee meetings, and the subsequent death of most of the Earth's population, as the wrangling continued indefinitely. If we applied this concept to the most important piece of private property we all own, our bodies, the system would fall apart immediately, as no one would be allowed to raise his arm to demonstrate approval at one of these meetings, let alone breathe, since we would all be owned by everyone else, and would have to seek their permission before doing any such thing.

Libertarianism is an aspect of political philosophy. It is separate and distinct from ethics. It does *not* address itself to what is right or wrong, moral or immoral. It confines itself solely to the issue of the justified and unjustified use of force. Take heroin use as an example. There are numerous theories of morality that denigrate such a practice. But as a libertarian, I must ask only one question: does placing such harmful substances in one's (adult) body, or buying or selling them, constitute a *per se* invasion? And the answer is clear: these acts do not fall outside the realm of legitimate acts in this political philosophy. As such, violence against those who engage in them is unjustified. To personally oppose the use of such drugs, yet reject physical sanctions against drug users sounds like a logical contradiction, but it is not.

This is just one of the hard cases, where people are engaging in activities that do not violate libertarian precepts, and yet they are largely reviled by much of society and/or threatened with violence, often in the form of imprisonment. Heroin usage is a perfect case in point. There are thousands of prisoners now incarcerated for this victimless crime of drug use. Not one of them has necessarily initiated violence; therefore, they deserve to be freed. (Anyone in this industry who has violated property or personal rights deserves punishment, but only for these acts, not for buying, selling or using these banned substances.) The present book, *Defending the Undefendable II: Freedom in All Realms,* is dedicated to discussing, analyzing and, most importantly, *defending* a whole host of economic actors innocent of violations of the libertarian code, yet they are under severe attack, either physically or intellectually. In many cases their actions are heroic, in that they persevere, even in the face of these unwarranted condemnations.

It is all well and good to promote libertarianism with regard to the "easy" cases. Books outlining the importance of privatization, deregulation, lower taxes, etc. are crucial. Articles showing the flaws of minimum wage laws, rent control and tariffs are a necessary part of the fight for liberty. And, some essays of this sort are included in the present work. But, sometimes, it is also important to ratchet up the pressure a bit: to show that not only is it desirable to rid ourselves of barriers to international trade, but, also, to give the smuggler his due; to demonstrate that not only is it desirous to deregulate the stock market, but it is also a legitimate part of the struggle to thank the inside trader, the corporate raider, and the multinational corporation for their heroic deeds.

Libertarianism is almost unique in that most people buy into its basic premises, but do not follow through to its logical conclusions. Who, after all, maintains that it is quite all right to go up to a non-aggressing stranger and physically accost him? To engage in rape, murder, theft, embezzlement? But this is precisely of what much modern legislation consists! Laws against heroin aggress against peaceful heroin users. Minimum wage laws violate the rights of those who disobey them; surely, it is not *per se* invasive to offer to hire someone for a mutually agreeable wage deemed too low by others. Rent control legislation penalizes people for setting prices on their own property.

Why, then, the need for a *Freedom in All Realms?* For one thing, you may not have noticed this, but we do not yet have a fully free pure libertarian society. Therefore, it is incumbent upon all of us to continue to strive mightily in that direction. One small contribution to this effort is to outline more and more hard cases; to demonstrate that libertarianism is a hardy weed, able to withstand all sorts of intellectual onslaughts against its basic premises, even difficult challenges. Another is educational. For some newcomers, the best way to introduce them to economic and social liberty is through a series of cases, starting with the easy basics and pretty much ending with them, while entirely eschewing the more and more radical instances of libertarianism. If you are looking for that sort of approach, *Defending the Undefendable II: Freedom in All Realms* is not the book for you. But for other neophytes, the only way to show them the merits of this philosophy is to also hit them with an (intellectual) bat right between the eyes. Hopefully, this book will merit that sort of description.

I have written this book in order to promote libertarianism. Too many people think that the only political options open to them are the left, liberal, nostrums offered by the Democratic party, or, the right, conservative ones offered by the Republicans. The former are relatively (but far from entirely) libertarian concerning personal liberties, such as the right to smoke marijuana, or to keep the prying eyes of the state out of the nation's bedrooms. But when it comes to economic liberties, the right to buy and sell, "truck and barter," engage in free enterprise, the party represented by the donkey is horrified. The party symbolized by the elephant, in contrast, is the very opposite: they oppose wage and price controls and some interventionistic regulations, and thus have some small adherence to laissez faire capitalism. But as far as personal liberties are concerned, they are bitterly opposed.

There is a third option, however. It is only the libertarian who favors human freedom in *all* realms of existence. Only the libertarian philosophy opposes imperialistic wars of aggression against nations that have not first invaded us. In sharp contrast, both Bush and Obama supporters favor aggressive wars in Iraq and Afghanistan, and the maintenance of some 800 U.S. military bases in about 150 different countries. That is hardly defense.

I chose the topics included in this volume because they all exemplify the libertarian premises of non-invasion and property rights. Most of them are my attempt to demonstrate the benefits of basic economic principles. Very few of them are relatively noncontroversial; what most of them have in common, however, is that they are like poking a (figurative) stick into the eye of the non-economist, and particularly the non-libertarian. Note to the general public: if you want a restful read, one that will not challenge your deeply held preconceptions in political economy, perhaps you should look elsewhere. I choose these topics because I am naturally confrontational. My formal courses in the teaching of economics are not aimed, so much, at getting the material across to my students. Instead, my modus operandi is to provoke the hell out of them, so that they will pick this up on their own. My aim here is similar: not so much to baby nonlibertarians into adopting this philosophy, as to get them so angry that they will challenge their fondly held beliefs. Then, too, there is a matter of internal education: not all those who call themselves libertarians are yet ready to accept the full implications of this perspective. Perhaps this book will gently help them along this path.

I think it is important for the general public to examine these controversial topics from a social/cultural point of view because libertarianism is the last best hope for a civilized life for mankind, indeed, for its very survival. It is the *only* philosophy predicated on the notion of "anything that is peaceful." Man may do *anything* he wishes, provided, only, that he respects the equal right of everyone else to do precisely the same thing. *All* other perspectives on political economy posit that it is all right to force innocent people to do things (e.g., pay taxes, exhibit passports, licenses, etc.) against their will, provided that someone in authority (the dictator, the democratically elected leader) approves. But, it is *barbaric* to compel innocent people to undertake acts of which they disapprove. This sort of compulsion when applied to domestic policy leads to unemployment, inflation, internal disarray. When applied to foreign policy it brings about unjustified wars. Given modern technology, the very future of our species is at stake, unless we adopt libertarianism. There can be nothing more important than that.

As in the case, I am sure, of all authors, it is my fervent hope that this book will have a strong impact. In the present case, that it will promote an understanding of this libertarian way of thinking on the part of the general public; that after reading this book they will no longer confuse libertarianism with libertinism, or liberalism; at best, that they will adopt this philosophy as their own and act so as to promote liberty. And, if not that, then they will at least no longer so bitterly oppose the freedom philosophy.

However, if past experience is any guide, the main response of the public will be utter revulsion. "How can you say that?"

"That is so cold and calculating," "But what about the poor?" "You have no human feelings" and charges of "economic illiteracy" will be the typical reaction. As if the poverty stricken in relatively capitalist countries—replete with cars, TV sets, air conditioning—are now immigrating en masse to the nations with greater economic interventionism. No, indeed, the traffic is pretty much all in the opposite direction. But, there will be those who will take to heart the challenges in this book; they will mull them over, do research on their own, and maybe, perhaps, just possibly, come to immerse themselves in the one and only ethical and true political economic philosophy.

The concept of "private property rights" and the principle of "non-aggression" are *not* the two main philosophies behind the logic of my thoughts presented here? No, those two are not the "main" perspectives under-girding this book. Rather, they are the *sole* and *only* ones doing so. Anything else is window dressing.

There are not any other key philosophies involved. No, none, nada, zero. Let us consider a few alternatives and see why all of them must be rejected. Libertarianism is sometimes confused with individualism, and a rejection of collectivism. The followers of Ayn Rand are particularly guilty of this obfuscation. Here, individualism is promoted and collectivism denigrated. But, there is nothing at all wrong with acting *collectively*, provided it is done on a voluntary basis. If it were really true that only individual action were legitimate, not cooperation between different individuals on a voluntary basis, then we would have to reject team sports such as football, basketball, baseball, as improper, while extolling the virtues, only, of individual sports, such as track, swimming, or arm wrestling. But singling out team sports is just plain silly.

Here is another one. It is sometimes claimed that jazz is the only libertarian music, while baroque, for example, is not. Why? Because in the former case, given certain very wide limitations, the musician is free to play pretty much whatever he wants, while in the latter, there is no latitude at all: the member of the orchestra must follow *exactly* what is in the score. And, not only that, all the strings must bow in unison. It is even worse for the winds; they must *breathe* exactly when the conductor allows. There can hardly be anything more intrusive than being told when to inhale or exhale. Even slave masters don't usually go in for that sort of thing. So is freedom of (musical) expression part of liberty? Of course not, as long as all members of the jazz entourage or string quartet engage in their pursuits free of threat, and no one has ever suggested this is not the case, both are free, *equally* free, insofar as political economy is concerned. One might as well say that Jackson Pollock had more liberty than Vincent van Gogh, since the former could spray paint on canvas seemingly willy-nilly, while the latter placed himself under great constraint. Again, this is frivolous.

Consider another case. It has sometimes been defined as ethical, indeed, as embodying the essence of morality, to embrace the notion: "From each according to his ability, to each according to his need." How does libertarianism react to this principle? Need it be rejected outright? No, not at all. As long as this concept is implemented by, and applied to, *only* those who agree with it, there is nothing incompatible with it and the doctrine that underlies this book. For example, the following voluntary institutions, to a greater or lesser extent, embrace this view: the nunnery, convent, kibbutz, commune, monastery, abbey, priory, friary, and any other religious community. Even the typical traditional family operates in this manner: the little girl eats in accordance with her needs, not her ability to earn money. So, there is nothing in the slightest incompatible with the embrace of this concept, and adherence to the libertarian principle.

Here is one last example. It is sometimes said that we should "live libertarianism." This is usually interpreted to mean that we should be nice, charitable, tolerant; we should embrace virtues of that sort. While there is nothing at all, certainly, incompatible between libertarianism on the one hand, and these characteristics on the other, there is also, equally, no requirement that libertarians embody them, either. There is no doubt that Ebenezer Scrooge could *also* incorporate the freedom philosophy. All he need do is act in accordance with the non-aggression axiom, based on private property rights. Apart from that, he could be as mean, bitter, nasty, intolerant, and uncharitable as he wished, with no tarnishing of his libertarian credentials whatsoever.

of international cooperation, specialization, and a worldwide division of labor.

We see this clearly in the case of maple syrup and bananas (see the attached table on absolute advantage towards the end of this chapter). Sure, bananas could be produced in Canada. All it would take is thousands, or perhaps hundreds of thousands, of gigantic and stupendously costly hothouses. And just as certainly, a tropical country such as Costa Rica could produce maple syrup. They could do this by erecting large refrigerators, in which they would keep their maple trees. (We're talking big refrigerators here.)

The very idea is ludicrous, of course. We all see the fallacy. Far better for the Canadians to produce maple syrup, for the Costa Ricans to grow bananas, and for each to trade for the item the other specializes in — to mutual advantage. What is the best way for a piano teacher to get a car? To build one herself? Or, to give piano lessons, and purchase an auto with the proceeds? To ask this is to answer it: of course, she should stick to what she does well, and not foray off into the very uncertain world (for her) of vehicle manufacture. Very few people, however, see that the same principle applies to textiles, shoes, autos, and electronic goods like television sets. Indeed, to *everything* under the sun. But it does, it does.

Consider textiles for a moment. If buyers are offered the choice between a locally made pair of denim jeans for fifty dollars and an identical one manufactured in Southeast Asia — Hong Kong, let us say — for ten dollars, there is little doubt that virtually all consumers will choose to be thrifty and save forty of their hard-earned dollars. And the inevitable result will be the loss of domestic jobs in denim production.

But let us not stop here, as do the protectionists: for there are several more effects to be considered. What, pray tell, will the consumers do with that extra forty dollars? They may spend it on other local products, and if they do, some of the now unemployed denim workers can find jobs in these other lines.

I. TRADE

1.

THE MULTINATIONAL ENTERPRISER

As never before, multinational corporations are under attack both at home and abroad. Foreign host governments have imposed a panoply of restrictions including export and import quotas, limitations on remittance of profits, convertibility controls, demands for participation in management, requirements that foreign nationals be hired, and mandatory reinvestment of earnings. Lurking in the background is the ever present threat of nationalization and expropriation—with inadequate compensation, of course.

Here at home . . . well, just recall the huge public protests whenever the World Trade Organization meets. Multinational firms are accused of exporting jobs and thus creating unemployment; of avoiding their fair share of taxes and thus placing burdens on those who are less able to pay. They are charged with exploiting underdeveloped countries, monopolizing, profiteering, and ruining our balance of payments. It sometimes almost appears that they are accused of everything bad under the sun, with the possible exceptions of bad breath and body odor.

The charge is often made, both here and abroad, that the size, wealth, power, mobility, and efficiency of international

3

enterprise places it beyond the sovereign control of any nation. Thus a Frankenstein monster of business, one that is not an ordinary corporate citizen, is said to be aborning and is or will soon be a law unto itself.

Not unexpectedly, the response to this sort of thinking has been fear, suspicion, and resentment. Dozens of governments around the world are proposing or creating laws with the express purpose of emasculating these firms.

Despite this well orchestrated assault, I do not find the case against multinational enterprisers compelling. I see little justification for the great and ever growing number of constraints placed on international commerce. On the contrary, I look upon this movement with great trepidation. I fear that if it succeeds, we shall witness the passing of an institution that is uniquely capable of preserving an international division of labor, worldwide trade, and the tranquility that must always accompany such universal economic cooperation.

Let us make no mistake about this. For no less than the future of world peace may depend upon decisions we will have to make over the next several years in this regard.

One of the most important determinants of success in the quest for peace will be our ability to bridge the gap between the "have" and the "have not" nations. Great disparities in wealth have always been a source of envy and jealousy, a destabilizing phenomenon in world affairs. But private international business firms, unlike our multitudinous governmental give-away programs, have been one of the very few successful forces contending with large international wealth differentials. World-based corporations bring new technologies, education, training, and higher wages to the underdeveloped areas of the world. More important, they bring a realistic hope and expectation that important progress can be made.

Let us consider then, in some detail, several of the most often mentioned criticisms leveled against international corporations.

In this way, we can show just how flimsy is the case against these firms.

The complaint is often made that American companies are responsible for "exporting" jobs and should be stopped. For example, employment loss is blamed on investment abroad, on imports from foreign parents of American corporations, on the transfer of our technology to other countries, and on the growth of multinational corporations, which are said to be responsible for all these factors.

There are serious flaws in this argument. If it is true that American investment overseas creates unemployment here, then it must be equally true that investment in one state by a company located in another ought to create unemployment in the company's home state. If an investment by Ford in Germany causes unemployment in the United States, then an investment by a Los Angeles company in Texas must cause unemployment in California. If one should be prohibited, so should the other. Neither prohibition, however, is acceptable.

The analysis can be carried still further. If it is true for a nation and a state, then it must be true for a city, a neighborhood, and even a street. To carry this argument to its logical conclusion, we must say that any resident of Elm Street who invests on River Street deprives his neighbors of employment; and that these Elm Street neighbors have as much justification to prohibit his export of capital to River Street as the government has to shackle the foreign investment policies of worldwide corporations. If carried to its logical conclusion, the opposition to foreign investment would prevent any individual investing with anyone else! (Note the parallels between this case and international trade.)

But it is not true that American concerns have decreased domestic employment. The fact is that very little of the foreign production undertaken by parents of American corporations would have been possible to launch domestically. Such activity would have had to surmount foreign tariff barriers,

5

import controls, and transportation costs. Like it or not, the choice faced by our companies is not between creating jobs here with local production or creating jobs overseas with production abroad. Rather, it is often between our building a foreign plant or not building one at all, anywhere—and losing out to foreign competition. Any attempt, therefore, to throttle the American firm in the hope of shifting jobs to our country is not likely to succeed.

And it is misleading to think about employment solely in quantitative terms. International enterprises play a far more important role than that of merely increasing the number of jobs at home. The goal of economic policy is not simply an increase in employment *per se*. If it were, we could reach it overnight by merely tearing up the roads between New York and Los Angeles, and hiring workers to carry the usual load of freight on their backs in the form of 50 pound sacks. This would keep us "fully employed" (and impoverished) for the next 10,000 years.

Every new labor saving device destroys jobs. But this is of great benefit to mankind. It frees labor for tasks that were impossible to accomplish previously! At the time of the founding of our nation, more than 95 percent of the labor force had to work on the farm to keep us fed; nowadays, less than 5 percent is so employed. Had we known that this would happen, should we have worried about the loss of jobs in agriculture? Should we have tried to stop the advances in technology that obliterated 90 percent of the jobs in existence at the time? On the contrary, it was the freeing of 90 percent of the labor force from farm work that allowed us to take the gigantic steps forward we have made in the past two centuries.

So it is not just any old employment, but *productive* employment, that is the goal of economic policy. And here is where international firms come in. For all the hue and cry against them, these companies are unequaled masters of creating the most productive employment the world has ever known. Before their entrance on the scene, the deployment of labor to its most productive uses was all but limited to a single nation. Now it has been widened to include the entire world.

Should space travel ever become commercially feasible, there will undoubtedly arise multiplanetary corporations, which will earn profits by carrying the principles of comparative advantage to the very edges of the universe. Although the complainers of the future will protest that the multiplanetary corporations are exporting jobs to Mars, or some such nonsense, universal well-being will be maximized, not harmed, by a system that allows Martians and Earthlings to do what they do best, and then to trade with one another; and one which allows a corporation formed on one planet to have subsidiaries on the other.

A related complaint made against international corporations is that they open plants in foreign countries in order to take advantage of cheap labor. The issue seems particularly galling to unions in this country. Worse, the business community is in such a state of disarray on this question that many spokesmen who ought to know better have actually conceded the need for remedial legislation—laws, that is, that would hamper the opening of branches in low-wage areas.

First of all, it is impossible for international corporations to take advantage of low-wage laborers. A corporation can only offer a wage above, below or equal to the one prevailing before it came upon the scene. If the offered wage is higher, the worker must gain; if lower, he need not accept the offered employment; if the same, his condition is unchanged, except that he now has one additional option that was previously unavailable to him. In no case, then, can the labor force of the undeveloped country be exploited except by being offered and by accepting better wage scales. If this be "exploitation," this is exactly what is needed in the Third World. Far from exploiting underdeveloped countries, international firms have done more than anyone else, including all the world welfare

"SORRY, KID, I'M OFF TO SRI LANKA—I CAN
GET A SHINE THERE FOR ABOUT SIX CENTS."

organizations put together, to drag them forward into the twenty-first century. Indeed, the main complaint heard from the underdeveloped world is that they receive too little multinational investment, not that they receive too much.

Nor are the multinational companies' foreign hiring practices motivated only by a search for cheap labor, although that is no doubt a significant part of the equation. The most often mentioned reasons for foreign investment are savings on transportation costs, proximity to raw materials and markets, avoidance of quotas, tariffs, and excessive taxation, procurement of foreign skills and technology, and any other advantages offered by host governments.

But even if foreign investment in low-wage areas were to occur on a massive scale, new employment would arise here to take the place of the work farmed out. Although this may be difficult to comprehend at a time of high and persistent unemployment, it is true. The reasons for our present high unemployment rate are many and complex, but they do not include the hiring of cheap foreign labor. The proof? If foreign labor is truly cheaper than domestic, even when productivity and all other economic differentials are taken into account, then costs would have to fall if an American corporation were to fire some of its workers at home in order to hire cheaper ones abroad. In turn, prices to the consumer would decrease, output would expand and profits would rise. Any of these consequences—and certainly the combination of all three—would create jobs here.

Consider a decrease in the final price of the goods. Consumers who would have been willing to buy the product at the old price, now have extra money in their pockets. Some of this will be saved, creating jobs in construction, basic industries and investment, depending upon how the money is loaned out by banks. Some of it will be spent in this country for unrelated goods, creating new job opportunities in other fields. And some of the money will be spent to buy more of the same good. This, along with the extra purchases by people who had not bought any at the old, higher price, will insure the expansion of output. But more output requires more workers.

The higher profits will be distributed, in part, to the stockholders, increasing their purchasing power. This spending will create new jobs for those displaced by foreign labor. Non-distributed profits will be retained by the corporation for internal expansion. This, too, will create employment opportunities for American workers.

The spending that is done abroad will not immediately help domestic employment. But eventually, when the foreigners use their earnings, some of the money will flow back to the United States and create export jobs here.

Although it is impossible to pinpoint exactly where the new jobs will come from—new consumer spending, product expansion, profits, increased international trade—we can, with perfect certainty, conclude that they will come. For the number of employment slots that need to be filled is not finite and fixed for all time. A job is the manifestation of unmet consumer desire. As long as people want more than they have, there will be work to be done and opportunities for employment. This is the only possible explanation of the fact that more than 95 percent of our present jobs did not exist 200 years ago! Thus there is no reason to fear our employment of low-paid foreign labor. We, along with them, can only gain from cooperation, an international division of labor, and trade.

In addition, if multinationals are forbidden to start affiliates in the low-wage underdeveloped world, the totalitarians will more easily be able to make inroads and spread their sphere of influence, assuming the contrary to fact conditional that the U.S. is itself not the leading imperialist power in the world today. We are locked in a competitive ideological struggle with the forces of totalitarianism the world over—a battle the free world seems to be losing among the neutralist countries. It makes precious little sense to strip ourselves of one of our most effective weapons in our struggle with totalitarianism: our ability to demonstrate to these nations—by involving them in it—the benefits of our free enterprise system. (OK, ok, of what remains of the little economic freedom we once had; at the time of this writing, we have witnessed four years of the socialistic-fascist Bush, and almost two years of the socialistic-fascist Obama.)

Then, there is the charge of hypocrisy. Would anyone propose a domestic policy of not hiring the poor? Hardly. Public policy in the United States is at least ostensibly devoted to helping the poor: millions of dollars spent on job training, specialized schooling and other programs attest to that. Nor can men of good will object to the opening of a new plant in any of the deprived areas of our own country, in the Appalachians or the Deep South or the inner cities of Newark and Detroit.

Yet, opposition to employment of foreign low-wage labor is surely the moral equivalent of these policies.

A word about business excesses. Yes, there are dishonest businessmen. And it is the duty of all of us to constantly strive to keep our own houses in order. But a few legitimate complaints have been allowed to smear the very idea of international enterprise, and this is wrong. There is also a good bit of confusion, both within and outside the economic community, as to what constitutes business malpractice.

For example, the attempt to prohibit multinational enterprise from taking advantage of "tax havens" is a dubious one. The objection is to the fact that the business concerns take the tax structures of several countries into account before opening a new plant, and, other things being equal, are more than likely to pick the one with the lowest taxes. But the tax burden is one of the many factors that every rational business must take into consideration. If anything, the countries of the world will benefit from the healthy winds of competition in tax policies. Let the world marketplace take a hand in reining in some of the more outlandish national tax policies!

To summarize, far from being the international bogeymen often depicted in the media, multinational corporations are a force for growth, prosperity, and progress—*especially* among the nations of the Third World, which are in the greatest need of economic development. Our thinking on these issues needs to be seriously reconsidered.

2.

THE SMUGGLER

A smuggler is a person who imports goods without paying the taxes (usually known as customs duties or tariffs) imposed on these goods by government. He also transfers goods whose importation or exportation has been forbidden entirely by government.

But ought government to be prohibiting any sort of international trade? Should the state impose any sorts of taxes on the goods that cross national boundaries?

There is a lot of talk nowadays about free trade. But this very concept tends to drive political leaders into such a tizzy of fear that they substitute it with phrases like "freer trade" or "enhanced trade" or "fair trade" or some other such circumlocution. In that way the dread name never has to pass their lips in its pure form.

We the people, however, need not labor under this apprehension. Instead, we would do well to understand the theory of free trade, in all its pristine glory, and realize that it is in the best interests of the people.

The United States, the land of the free and the home of the brave, is supposed to be the bastion of free enterprise in this regard. The less said about this during the Bush (I and II) and Obama administrations, the better. But even during the presidency of Ronald Reagan, who constantly crooned about the "magic of the marketplace" in solving economic problems and bringing prosperity to all, the United States was far from a living embodiment of the principles of Adam Smith. In point of fact, the United States is a rather protectionist country even under the rule of those who employ free trade rhetoric. And in recent years, it has increased tariffs or set quotas on a wide range of goods and products, including motorcycles, steel, autos, and textiles.

Yet self-imposed banishment from the benefits of specialization and the international division of labor is a serious mistake even for a large country like the United States, which contains within its own borders a global-scale market, many skills and raw materials and much of the world's available capital; for small nations to pursue such policies, is folly indeed.

The very term "protectionist" is a vast misnomer. It implies that the citizens are being defended against economic exploitation which is somehow made even more sinister by its foreign genesis. In fact, nothing could be further from the truth.

In order to see this clearly, let us start not with a nation which refuses to trade with others, but with an individual who sets up trade barriers between himself and all other people. Such a person, of course, will have to provide for all of his needs: for each and every one of them. He will have to grow his own food, make and mend his own clothing, build a house for himself, minister to himself when he falls ill, entertain himself, etc. Not being able to specialize in any one thing, his productivity will not be able to attain livable levels. His life will be "nasty, brutish and short." If everyone tried the path of economic solipsism, this fertile Earth, which today can support the lives of more than six billion people, might possibly be able to keep at most a few million snarling savages living on a miserable, semi-starvation basis.

On a national level, one argument for protectionism is that a policy of free trade would mean the loss of domestic jobs. Those who fear elimination of all government-imposed barriers to trade cite prospective job losses in such callings where foreigners can produce goods at a fraction of the local costs. And this is indeed realistic. An end to laws which protect such industries from foreign competition would mean a wholesale cutback—or perhaps even an entire elimination—of employment in these sectors.

But this is all to the good. For why should precious local labor be expended on jobs which produce less than they might? The farmer who works at tasks that could be done as well by an animal or by mechanical means (plowing, hauling, lifting) will have less to show for his efforts than if he concentrated on doing things that he could do far better (running a mechanical plow, hauling by tractor, using a forklift). In just the same manner, and for the same reasons, locals would be far better off if people now employed in producing domestic products on an inefficient basis shifted themselves into job slots where they could be more productive.

For "any old employment" cannot and should not be our goal. Millions of farm jobs, heck, billions of them for that matter, could be created if people used teaspoons to dig up our rich earth, instead of plowing. What we want, what we *need*, as a country if we are to successfully negotiate our economic way into the twenty-first century, are jobs in which people are freed up to do more productive things.

This was the free trade message of Adam Smith, who inveighed against the mercantilists, the economic "nationalists" of his day. He saw clearly that the "wealth of nations" was dependent upon productivity, that is, labor directed to its most efficient employment. And as a necessary corollary, he demonstrated that this could only take place under a regime of full free trade, where government placed no obstacles in the way of international cooperation, specialization, and a worldwide division of labor.

We see this clearly in the case of maple syrup and bananas (see the attached table on absolute advantage towards the end of this chapter). Sure, bananas could be produced in Canada. All it would take is thousands, or perhaps hundreds of thousands, of gigantic and stupendously costly hothouses. And just as certainly, a tropical country such as Costa Rica could produce maple syrup. They could do this by erecting large refrigerators, in which they would keep their maple trees. (We're talking *big* refrigerators here.)

The very idea is ludicrous, of course. We all see the fallacy. Far better for the Canadians to produce maple syrup, for the Costa Ricans to grow bananas, and for each to trade for the item the other specializes in—to mutual advantage. What is the best way for a piano teacher to get a car? To build one herself? Or, to give piano lessons, and purchase an auto with the proceeds? To ask this is to answer it; of course, she should stick to what she does well, and not foray off into the very uncertain world (for her) of vehicle manufacture. Very few people, however, see that the same principle applies to textiles, shoes, autos, and electronic goods like television sets; indeed, to *everything* under the sun. But it does, it does.

Consider textiles for a moment. If buyers are offered the choice between a locally made pair of denim jeans for fifty dollars and an identical one manufactured in Southeast Asia— Hong Kong, let us say—for ten dollars, there is little doubt that virtually all consumers will choose to be thrifty and save forty of their hard-earned dollars. And the inevitable result will be the loss of domestic jobs in denim production.

But let us not stop here, as do the protectionists, for there are several more effects to be considered. What, pray tell, will the consumers do with that extra forty dollars? They may spend it on other local products, and if they do, some of the now unemployed denim workers can find jobs in these other lines.

They may save the money instead, but then the banks will be able to make loans on easier terms, thus creating additional jobs in domestic construction, home building, and heavy industry. Alternatively, they may purchase four additional pairs of foreign jeans (or other imports from other countries) for that same fifty dollars.

So we must now ask, what will the foreign suppliers do with the ten dollars (or the fifty dollars) paid to them by the people in the domestic country? American dollars are no more acceptable in Hong Kong than are dollars of that Chinese colony in the U.S. If the new owners of these American dollars want to use them, there is only one place in the world, ultimately, where they are acceptable: the home country. And when these funds come back to our nation, they will be for the purchase of goods and services. And that will create still additional jobs here.

If the inhabitants of Hong Kong are perverse, and refuse to spend their American dollars here—if they stuff them in mattresses or burn them, for example—this will *greatly* benefit our economy. For by this policy, they would present us with valuable commodities and receive in return pieces of paper which their own actions had rendered worthless. It would be as if Hong Kong had granted the U.S. a gift, or foreign aid, consisting of denim jeans. And it could hardly hurt the Americans to be the recipients of such largesse. (If the Hong Kong exporters spent their U.S. currency in a third country where they were acceptable to certain sellers, such as France, then the French would either turn around and spend the funds in America, creating jobs here, or keep them, in effect making a free gift to us.) This form of "foreign aid" would, of course, make our denim industry superfluous, but all citizens saving on their clothing bills would now be able to afford additional goods—and new jobs would be created in the industries catering to these new desires.

No matter how you slice it, trade between consenting adults benefits both parties to the deal. Otherwise it would not take place. The exchange of U.S. dollars for Hong Kong denim is no exception.

Nor is the exchange of U.S. dollars for cloth and clothing from the People's Republic of China. Yet, a major dispute erupted only a few years ago between those two nations, with Peking threatening to retaliate against Washington for U.S. protectionist interference with textile trade. According to the official Chinese news agency, Xinhua, the Chinese ambassador was unhappy with the U.S. "country of origin" rules. Under these regulations, U.S. customs agents had been authorized to reject clothing manufactured in Hong Kong but based on materials and semi-completed garments originating in mainland China. The Chinese protested that this rule would threaten several billion dollars worth of textile exports to the U.S. A spokesman said that "hundreds of factories and about sixty thousand jobs would be harmed in [his country's] southern provinces alone, and this would be a grievous blow to China's industry, employment, trade, and economic development."

Adam Smith must have been spinning in his grave. Imagine a country supposedly devoted to the principles of capitalism and free markets (that's us) erecting barriers to trade and the (ex?) communists (China) protesting!

The main sufferers from a policy of free trade, by the way, are not the lower paid workers with generalized training, which is as applicable to denim production as to anything else. They will find alternative employment at comparable wages. The real losers are the protected factory owners, and the highly paid, heavily unionized workers with a great investment in skills specific to denim manufacture. It is mainly they who will suffer losses unless retrained. As a result, the unions typically support the manufacturers in their bid for more protection and more assistance.

One of the biggest limitations on further exports from North America to the less developed countries is the fact that they don't have enough dollars with which to buy our exports. And they can't get our currency unless we allow them to trade with us. Foreign aid, the time-honored socialistic alternative solution to Third World poverty, is not the answer. Experience and logic suggests that "aid" money will only be used to purchase limousines for the rulers, weapons to keep them in power, useless steel mills and statues to promote their vain glory (the three M's: machine guns, monuments, and Mercedes) and money with which to further centralize and socialize their economy and thus plunge the people into further and deeper misery. The motto for those really concerned with the plight of the downtrodden Third World peoples ought to be: "millions in foreign trade, not a penny in foreign aid."

If another country can make denim more cheaply than we can, it makes sense to concentrate on what we do best, allow them to do the same, and then to trade—utilizing the special skills and factor endowments of each region of the globe. We will never be as rich a nation as we could be if we force people to work at jobs others can do more cheaply. The high-priced lawyer who insists on doing all his own typing, office cleaning and errand running will soon learn that he can do far better solely as an attorney (see table attached at the end of this chapter). The tragedy is that our country continues to waste valuable labor inputs on tasks that can only be considered menial—from a worldwide and economic perspective.

There are other tragedies caused by protectionism, of course. One of them is the growth of something called "countertrade."

Suppose you had a used car that for some reason you no longer liked and you wanted instead to own a rowboat, a radio and a clock. In the ordinary course of events you would simply sell the automobile, whether through the want ads or to a used car dealer, take the money, and go out and purchase the rowboat, the radio and the clock. What could be more simple?

But suppose you were told that there was no money in society and that you would have to accomplish this task through barter. Do you have any idea how difficult that would be? Can you just imagine the odds of finding someone who wants a used car and has a rowboat, a radio, and a clock he wants to trade? In technical economic language, this is called the "double coincidence of wants." Economists use this phenomenon to show the importance of buying and selling with *money* because it would be a real coincidence indeed if such a trade could be conducted through barter.

But there is a fascinating change occurring in the international trade arena. It is called countertrade, and it's really only the bartering of one good, or set of goods or services, for another.

For example, Ford Motor Company of Detroit trades automobiles for Uruguayan sheepskins. Or Italy barters ships for Iraqi oil. Or Pierre Cardin receives Oriental silks in return for providing consulting services to China. Or a Mexican law firm gets woolen hats and noodles for giving legal advice to a Third World country.

Why have we been moving from trade, through the intermediation of money, to such international barter? One possibility is that with barter, countries can continue to import despite inadequate foreign exchange reserves and without risking additional balance of payments crises. This is a situation afflicting many Third World countries, which have, thanks to centralized and socialized planning, mismanaged their economies. Then too, countertrade is a way for these nations to deflect the austerity programs being imposed upon them by the International Monetary Fund, a lending source for the Third World made up of a consortium of institutions from the developed Western democracies.

A third reason is that bilateral countertrade arrangements can sometimes be used to evade tariff and non-tariff barriers to trade. If so, consider the plight of a country frozen out of a lucrative market in this manner. If it engages in countertrade, it will lose out through the inefficiency of barter. But it may make up for this, or perhaps even exceed it, by being able to jump over the tariff barrier.

The problem, in both these cases, is what economists call the "second best" solution. Barter may pay, but only because of governmental mismanagement or tariffs. The "first best" solution would be to bring the decentralized marketplace to the nations of the world, and to reduce or eliminate tariffs. Then, countertrade would no longer be needed, and the world could get back to more efficient utilization of the monetary system.

Another tragedy sometimes caused by protectionism is the flagrant waste of economic resources, other than labor, in order to get around government-imposed barriers to free trade. A case in point is the opening of Japanese auto plants in North America.

When I was a very young lad, my mother arranged a job for me with the neighborhood greengrocer. I was to count the string beans filled to the brim of a very large bin. The purpose of this "employment," of course, was not to create a good or service, or to help with sales or promotion or to be productive in any of the usual senses of that word. Rather, this "job" was a disguised form of babysitting, and my wage was a negative one: my mother paid the grocer to keep me busy and out of her hair. (Some of my detractors have gone so far as to wish me similar employment in my adulthood.)

In like manner, this opening of a new automobile manufacturing plant cannot be understood as a typical business decision. True, the factory *resembled* those built for economic reasons. But this resemblance was only coincidental. The only reason for the location of this plant was to hop over the steep tariff wall imposed on Japanese and other foreign cars, and to escape various non-tariff barriers erected in front of importers of such cars by the domestic authorities. In a word, the government succeeded—through extortion—in forcing the Japanese to build a plant they would never have agreed to build otherwise.

As a nation, we should hang our heads in shame that such an evil deed was perpetrated in our names. The location of this plant was not based on efficiency grounds, nor can it possibly accomplish this end. One need only consider the fact that a significant amount of the output of this plant is shipped back to Japan for assembly. That being the case, it follows that these companies would have been able to more cheaply produce their cars with an additional (equivalent) plant in Japan, rather than this one. As a result of bullying, these manufacturers have produced a more costly product, and American consumers have had to pay higher prices for their automobiles.

Since this bit of economic coercion, we have been perceived as even more interventionistic and, thus, even more inhospitable to foreign investment. As well, to a greater degree than before, we have been seen as a country that cannot attract foreign investment on its own merits, and instead must resort to economic strong-arm tactics to achieve this end.

Why is it, then, if the case for free trade makes so much sense, that we nonetheless find ourselves barricaded from greater affluence by high tariff walls?

Part of the answer seems to be that too often even those who see how much sense free trade makes are overly concerned that it be not only free, but also "fair."

In the past few years, as a result, a new phrase has entered the common lexicon: "the level playing field." It sounds rather like sports jargon, but it is not. Instead it refers to a rather technical aspect of international trade. In this sense, the "level playing field" alludes to a situation in which the citizens of neither country have an unfair competitive advantage over the other. If trade between nations can be represented by a playing field, then, according to this doctrine, it should tilt neither one way nor the other, nor should the wind be at the back of either team, or the sun more in the eyes of one side than the other.

"EXCUSE ME, LADIES AND GENTLEMEN, IT'S THREE O'CLOCK,
TIME TO CHANGE SEATS SO THAT THE U.S. TRADE DELEGATION
FACES THE SUN."

In sports such as football, basketball, hockey, and soccer, the goals are switched around halfway through the match so as to equalize any disadvantage which might result from an uneven playing field.

The practice of greatest concern to advocates of the level playing field in international trade is that of subsidizing exports. U.S. advocates of the level playing field, for example, have worried a lot in recent years about the cheap fish sent to their country from Canada. This is a result, they contend, of Canada's unemployment insurance scheme, which pays people all winter for what is only a summer job. In the view of these U.S. worrywarts, this is only a thinly disguised form of subsidy for Canadian fishermen, one that harms their own maritime industry. For without this advantage, the fishing industry to our north would not be able to compete so efficiently. Therefore, U.S. trade negotiators have demanded a "level playing field," on which the Canadian government does not help its citizens to compete "unfairly" against Americans.

In a superficial analysis, this point of view is reasonable. After all, there are specific losers—the New England fishermen—who suffer directly from Canadian unemployment insurance. But if we look a little deeper, we can see that insisting on a "level playing field" makes no economic sense at all. In order to prove this, let us not dwell on situations where Canadian bureaucrats pursue a policy which, in effect if not by intention, allows citizens of that country to sell products more cheaply to Americans than would otherwise be possible. Let us consider instead an extreme hypothetical case in which that government encourages or even compels its citizens to *give away* their goods to Americans free of charge!

For example, suppose that a law were passed tomorrow permanently subsidizing at the rate of one hundred, ten percent of all free gifts of lumber to the United States. That is, for every $100 worth of wood products Canadian citizens sent across the border at a zero price, the Canadian government would give those citizens $110. Pass lightly over the objection that this would bankrupt our northern neighbor in short order, and ask only what effect this would have on the economy of the United States.

Here, it is easy to see that although this policy would drive into bankruptcy the entire U.S. forest industry, in would be a *boon* to the U.S. economy as a whole. For now, the Americans could have just as much wood as before, compliments of Canada, while freeing up large numbers of workers and whatever capital could be transferred to other occupations. Our standard of living would therefore rise, with no additional inputs on our part. This is roughly how the war-torn economies of Europe were rebuilt after World War II, thanks to the generosity of Marshall Plan aid. If they wished to remain logically consistent, the Americans could hardly turn around now and refuse such aid, were it offered to them.

For this is all the "uneven" playing field consists of: an offer from one country to subsidize the economy of another. Instead of objecting to other nations pursuing such policies, each should *encourage* others to "tilt" the playing field in the direction of subsidizing exports. And yet, the conventional economic wisdom in North America holds the very opposite, i.e., that each nation should protest when its neighbors subsidize it.

Lunacy is not to be found only in the psychiatric wards. Nor, unfortunately, is it limited to the advocates of the level economic playing field. It is every bit as prevalent among economic nationalists, those who claim that free trade threatens the cultural identity, or, even worse, the political sovereignty of any nation that dares to embrace it. A while ago we heard much absurd talk of the Japanese "invasion" of North America—a reference to the sale of cars, stereo components, computers, and other goods within North America by Japanese companies. We have heard even more asinine assertions that the Japanese have belatedly taken our victory over their forces in World War II away from us, using economic, rather than military, means to do so.

But what about the arts? Under free trade, music and art and culture from other countries will come swooping in, it is charged, and will overcome the homegrown variety. Nonsense. It is silly to think that only homegrown art can express the culture of a nation. Mozart and Bach were not Americans. The Bible, the works of Shakespeare and Rembrandt were not composed in the Land of the Free, Home of the Brave.

Consider the following illustration of what economists call "absolute advantage." We assume two years, two products and two countries. If there is no trade between the two countries, Canada will produce 500 units of maple syrup and 15 bananas for a GDP of 515 (we make the simplifying assumption that these two items can be added up). Costa Rica will grow 400 bananas and 25 maple syrup units for a GDP of 425.

Table I	Absolute advantage		
	Maple Syrup	Bananas	GDP
Canada	500	15	515
Costa Rica	25	400	425
No trade	525	415	940
Trade	1,000	800	1,800

World GDP (consisting of just these two countries) will be 940, figured either as the total of all bananas (415) and all maple syrup buckets (525), or as the addition of the GDPs of these two countries (515 + 425). In the last line, we depict what happens when trade between these two nations opens up, and each spends both "years" on the product in which it has an absolute advantage. Canada doubles its annual production of 500 maple syrup bottles to 1,000, eschewing bananas entirely, and Costa Rica puts all its resources into bananas, ignoring the other product, and doubles its previous output of 400 to 800. World GDP rises from 940 to almost double, at 1,800. Surely, both countries are better off under such an arrangement; if not, they can always refuse to trade, and return to the economic autarky of the first iteration.

Table II	Comparative Advantage		
	Wheat	TV Sets	GDP
U.S.	125	300	425
Japan	200	1,500	1,700
No trade	325	1,800	2,125
Trade	250	3,000	3,250

But suppose one nation is "better" at producing *all* products. Does the case for full free trade fall apart? It does not. In order to see this, we introduce the concept of comparative advantage, where one country is more efficient than another across the board. Again, we assume two "years," two products and two countries. Only this time we endow one of these nations with an absolute advantage in *both* products. Here, the supermen from Japan can produce more wheat than we can in America and, also, more televisions! Let us go through the numbers. With no trade, U.S. GDP consists of 125 bushels of wheat and 300 televisions, for a total of 425 (again, we make the simplifying assumption that these apples and oranges can be meaningfully added up). Japan produces 200 wheat units and 1,500 televisions, for a GDP of 1,700. There are 325 bushels of wheat in existence at the end of the two-year period and 1,800 TV sets, for a world GDP of 2,125 = 325 wheats + 1,800 TVs, or a GDP of 425 in the U.S. and 1,700 in Japan.

Now, in the second round of analysis, again trade between the two occurs. This time, each country specializes in the item for which it has a comparative advantage (remember, Japan has an absolute advantage in both items, so this cannot be used to generate trade). So, who has a comparative advantage

27

in what? Japan is five times better than us in television manufacture, but only 1.6 times better than its American counterparts in wheat. Or, to turn this around, the U.S. can produce 62.5% of the amount of wheat forthcoming from Japan, but only 20% of the TV sets. So, Japan has a comparative advantage in the electronic equipment, and the U.S. has a comparative advantage in farm goods. In the fourth line, we see the results of this sort of specialization. America pulls out of electronic manufacturing and throws all of its energies into farming. If we can produce 125 wheat units with half of our resources, we can attain 250 if we will focus on this product; Japan, too, can double its TV production from 1,500 to 3,000 sets if it focuses solely on that product. As a result of this trade between two very different countries, one "developed," the other not, world GDP rises from 2,125 to 3,250, a gigantic increase attributable to this law of comparative advantage, discovered by David Ricardo in 1817. Would those modern politicians absorb this knowledge, which has been around some two centuries.

Consider one last numerical example of the benefits of trade, even between partners of very different circumstances. Here, we have a lawyer who can produce legal services at the rate of $1,000 per day, from which is generated $150 worth of secretarial services daily. If the lawyer works solo, he garners, after two days, $1,000 plus $150 for a total of $1,150. However, if the attorney obtains the help of a legal secretary, in the same two days he can earn $2,000 in court; and although he will have to pay his assistant $300 for the two days, he has still earned more than if he worked alone. When he subtracts $300 from the $2,000 he earned in court, he still has $1,700 left, which is more than the $1,150 he would have if he had worked alone at two occupations. Free trade benefits *both* parties, irrespective of their financial circumstances, QED.

Table III	More comparative advantage	
No Trade	Secretary	Lawyer
Day 1	150	1,000
Day 2	150	150
Total	300	1,150
Trade	Secretary	Lawyer
Day 1	150	1,000
Day 2	150	1,000
Total	300	2,000 − 300 = 1,700

3.

BRITISH PETROLEUM

British Petroleum (BP) is on everyone's list of bad guys. This makes them grist for our mill, as heroes. Heroes? How can we even *begin* to say that? On April 20, 2010, their Deepwater Horizon installation blew up, killing eleven employees, and unleashed more than 200 million gallons of oil into the Gulf of Mexico. This threatened the jobs, welfare and livelihoods of probably thousands of people living in Texas, Louisiana, Mississippi, Alabama, and Florida. Oil exploration is only the tip of the iceberg. There is also employment servicing this industry, plus tourism, food supply, fishing, etc. Not only does BP fail to deserve the honorific "heroic," but there is a serious question in the minds of many people as to whether or not the officers of this corporation should be considered outright criminals. Such, at least, is the case against BP.

Is there another side to this story? Yes, there is, although you will not hear it in the major media. Part of it consists of the realization that heavy industry (drilling, building, mining, exploring, dynamiting) is sometimes, heck, often *dangerous*. If you can't stand the heat, get out of these lines of work and become a librarian, teacher or shoe-shiner. For that reason alone, if for no other, the BP team ought to be congratulated. They take their lives and their property and put it on the line, every day.

But there is more. Why did BP place its Deepwater Horizon rig so far offshore (about 60 miles from the nearest land), and in such deep water (about 5,000 feet down)? Didn't they realize that drilling closer to, or over the continental shelf would have been safer? After all, it is easier to deal with calamities 50 feet below the water, than almost a mile straight down. Then, too, help is more readily available inshore. Of course, they did. But they were prevented from doing so by an unholy alliance of left-wing environmentalists and government regulators. As for the latter, the Minerals Management Service (MMS), they do not at all emerge unscathed from this imbroglio. They were involved in bribe taking, watching pornography on "company" time and on government computers, and taking drugs while on the job. This ought to give pause to all those who think that the solution for *any* problem at all, even one initially caused by government, is more regulation.

Nor does this even begin to acknowledge the full contribution of MMS to this imbroglio. According to *The Wall Street Journal*: "BP has come under heavy fire from Congress and environmental groups for its lack of readiness to handle a worst-case spill. But that criticism has overlooked a key fact: BP was required by federal regulators to base its preparations on Interior Department models that were last updated in 2004." These governmentally perpetrated models focused mostly on oil released onto the surface of the body of water, ignoring the effect of a deep-water spill.

We have not yet plumbed the depths of U.S. government responsibility for this mess. The Obama administration's thrall to the unions is so deep and so pervasive that several days after the oil spill, it declined the help of the Spill Response Group Holland, even though the capacity to deal with the problem by any one of their several ships offered was greater than all of ours together. The Dutch, leading experts in massive water problems, water management, and dike building, also offered to protect Gulf Coast marshlands with berms and sand barriers. This offer, too, was spurned. It was made on a no-cost basis, but, it would appear, the U.S. stuck to its principles for this sort of thing, and applied them as well to a dozen other offers of fleets of oil spill response vessels vastly superior to American alternatives.

Why is U.S. technology so behind? This is due to harmful environmental rules emanating from Washington, D.C. In the land of the free, home of the brave, salvage vessels are forbidden by law to put back into the sea oily water they have sucked up, if it is not at least 99.9985% pure. The technology of other nations is not so stringent as to require a standard of 15 parts per million. So, when U.S. ships gobble up contaminated water, they are forced to store it in onshore facilities. The long trips back to shore with each intake of water were time consuming, given the massive amounts of spewing oil. In contrast, Dutch vessels and those of other nations may have let more oil back into the Gulf, but would have been far more efficient.

Eventually, the U.S. government changed its tune (what happened to principles?) and accepted foreign help, but with a proviso. The Dutch couldn't use their superior methods, directly. Instead, they transferred their oil skimming equipment to U.S. boats. Why? As a sop to the unions; needless to say, this postponed cleanup efforts. As on the water, it was the same with the berm and sand-barrier efforts. Rather than allow the more efficient foreigners to have at it, their role was limited to the time-wasting training of U.S. organized labor.

Further, the "1990 Oil Protection Act" capped BP's financial responsibility for damages at $75 million. This cannot be squared with the tenets of laissez faire capitalism. (If and to the extent that this company was involved in creating this implicit subsidy for itself, it cannot be defended as a member in good standing of the free enterprise system. Rather, if true, it joins the ranks of the monopoly state of corporate capitalists, or fascists. But evidence to support this contention has not been brought forth, and the burden of proof rests with those who make such claims.) On the other hand, at the time of this writing the Obama administration is attempting to force this oil company to pay for the salaries lost due to the down time of all idled oil workers in the Gulf of Mexico. This would be bad enough. For, surely, to the extent this disaster was the responsibility of BP, the company should be held responsible for all direct damages to persons and property, with no cap at all. However, what makes this worse, far worse, is that the U.S. government wants to compel BP to pay for the lost salary of workers laid off due to the government's own moratorium on deepwater drilling.

The families of the workers killed in this tragedy are suing BP. Should they be able to collect? Not under libertarian law, at least. For these unfortunate people took it upon themselves to accept the responsibilities for their jobs. Presumably, they were paid an extra amount of salary in the form of hazardous duty pay to bear the additional risks that go with that type of employment. Should the heirs of those pilots who test new airplanes be allowed to sue for wrongful death? Not any more than in the BP case. Unless, that is, it can be proven that the officers of this oil company purposely blew up this installation, which is certainly not even alleged in this case.

Then, there is the Deep Water Royalty Relief Act of 1995 and the Outer Continental Shelf Lands Act, as amended in 1978. These are further governmental enactments that serve as a subsidy to the oil industry. They provide for relief from lease expenditures. The goal of the 1995 Act was, supposedly, to encourage the exploration for oil and natural gas production in the deep water areas of the Gulf of Mexico. Why was this needed? This is because oil production in this area was deemed by our central planners as too risky and expensive for private concerns to take on this challenge. If government policy makers are so intent upon promoting this activity, why don't they "man up" when something goes wrong with the results of their own decision making, instead of "looking for some butt to kick," as Obama announced recently. Were there any justice in the world, the President of the U.S. would look in the mirror for a suitable target for his boot.

No account of this human and environmental tragedy would be complete without a consideration of the evil Jones Act of 1920. Like the British Navigation Acts which were a part of the motivation for the secession of the U.S. from that country in 1776, these laws reserve for the domestic country the monopoly of shipping. Under Jones, only U.S. vessels can engage in commerce in U.S. waters such as the Gulf of Mexico, and they must be manned by U.S. crews. Yet, there were boats from other nations that were more than ready to help us in our hour of need, but they were turned back by the Coast Guard. Evidently, kowtowing to local unions—one of the main beneficiaries of the Jones Act—is more important to Obama than environmental considerations. One cannot help but remember that under Bush II, the Federal Emergency Management Agency (FEMA) also refused aid offered to New Orleans in the aftermath of Katrina. What is it with Washington, D.C., and the Gulf states?

There is also the Passenger Vessel Services Act (PVSA) of 1886 (46 U.S.C. 289) which provides that "no foreign vessel shall transport passengers between ports or places in the United States." Similar legislation in the airline industry prohibits foreign air carriers from transporting passengers from one U.S. city to another. The point is, it is all too easy to blame BP for the oil spill. With laws of this sort on the books, the U.S. government is at least partially responsible for this tragedy.

Another difficulty with this entire episode is that the Gulf of Mexico is either entirely unowned, and/or owned and controlled by the U.S. government. The former case gives rise to the tragedy of the commons, where the usual incentives to preserve and safeguard property are greatly if not entirely attenuated.

The latter corresponds to the Soviet economic system, where the government plans the whole economy. In contrast, were this body of water owned privately, say, by the Gulf of Mexico Corporation, it would then likely manage matters in a far superior manner. If they didn't, they would be subject to the usual market tests of profit and loss. In contrast, does Obama, personally, lose any money when oil is wasted, and/or comes to shore and ruins commerce there? Of course not.

Let us consider one objection to the foregoing. The Gulf of Mexico is (unlikely) owned by hundreds of corporations. One of them is particularly irresponsible: it allows a mining company to drill on its watery property, but imposes no strict safety regulations contractually (it can raise profits in that way). In the case of accident, it does not have anything like the necessary wherewithal to defray the costs to its neighboring aqueous owners. No insurance company will touch this fly-by-night operator with the proverbial ten-foot pole. What is the solution offered by the libertarian legal code to this disaster in the making? Why, an injunction would be granted against this ne'er do well in a split second, as it constitutes a clear and present danger, a threat. In order to safeguard itself from such legal suits, every owner of the Gulf would have an incentive to register his safety precautions with a court, or an association of owners.

So, the next time you hear someone blaming BP for this disaster, realize that the major, if not the entire culpability for this sad event belongs to the U.S. government, not to that oil company.

4.

NUCLEAR ENERGY

The deaths on April 20, 2010, pursuant to the explosion on British Petroleum's Deepwater Horizon oil rig, were a great tragedy. The blast killed eleven employees, and unleashed hundreds of millions of gallons of oil into the Gulf of Mexico.

That human and environmental tragedy provides all the more reason to re-examine the widely publicized misgivings about nuclear energy foisted upon us by the "ecology" movement.

The Deepwater Horizon tragedy was not, unfortunately, the first energy-related accident to claim numerous lives. Rather, the non-nuclear energy field has been plagued with a series of similar disasters.

Other offshore oil drilling rig mass fatalities include:

- the deaths of eighty-four men with the sinking of the oil drilling rig Ocean Ranger off Newfoundland;
- the capsizing of the ten thousand-ton Alexander Kielland accommodation rig off Norway in the North Sea in March 1980, with the catastrophic loss of 123 lives;
- a November 1979 oil rig collapse during a storm in the Bohai Gulf off northeast China, which killed 72 workmen;

- a blowout in October 1980 of the U.S.-owned rig Tappmeyer off Saudi Arabia in which 18 people perished.

Coal mining, too, has been marred by numerous large-scale accidents, the world over:

- in Canada, the Nova Scotia coal mine "Springhill" was the site of a disaster that claimed 39 lives in 1956 and another 74 in 1958;
- in the U.S., roughly 300 coal miners die in the line of duty every year;
- in addition to cave-ins, coal miners have long been subject to the dreaded "black-lung" disease which has crippled many, and, directly or indirectly, killed many others.

If this past record looks bleak, the future bodes ill as well. Despite ever-improving technologies, as the quest for offshore oil continues apace into evermore inhospitable environments, the only rational expectation is for more of the same.

The same holds true for coal mining. If energy prices continue their recently interrupted upward path, one source of additional coal supplies may be to dig deeper—into increasingly more dangerous terrain. Strip-mining of coal nearer to the surface brings in its wake the risk of water runoffs and slides and other hazards—vociferously pointed out to us by the self-styled "ecologists." And other alternative energy supplies come with dangers of their own. A hydroelectric dam eruption that drowned thousands of people in India is a chilling case in point.

What of nuclear power? Despite the widespread media-ted wailing and gnashing of teeth that accompanied the meltdown at Three Mile Island in Pennsylvania, the plain fact is that not a single solitary radiation-related death has occurred in the quarter century of commercial nuclear power generation. As the famous bumper sticker has it: "More people died at Chappaquiddick than at Three Mile Island."

And yet the litany goes on. Protesters at nuclear power stations continually attempt to halt operations—and are accorded

"...BAD NEWS, TOM. I JUST GOT OFF THE PHONE WITH THE GOVERNOR. HE TURNED DOWN YOUR REQUEST FOR NON-NUCLEAR POWER TO RUN THE ELECTRIC CHAIR."

a respectful-to-fawning hearing by the nation's press. Although trespassers on private property, the protesters are given credit for "morality" and "concern."

Now, this is not to say that the government should place its big fat thumb on the scale and tip the economy in the direction of nuclear power. Not at all. It should not have any dog in this fight; it should pick no favorites at all. In this regard, the Price-Anderson Act, which limits liability in the case of a mishap in this industry, should be repealed forthwith. If and to the extent that oil and coal are guilty of property rights violations in the form of trespassing smoke particles, this should be stopped. The libertarian response is thus one of fair competition. Allow all of the energy sources, oil, coal, nuclear, wind, solar, water, wind, etc., to compete with each other, without fear or favor. And let the market decide which ones, and in what proportions, will best serve mankind. That is the way we do things, roughly, with fruits and vegetables, or, at least, the way we *should* manage these competing foodstuffs (don't remind me of sugar subsidies, taxes on beer, regulations of "fatty" foods, etc.).

Why not for energy sources too?

5.

THE CORPORATE RAIDER

In 1932, Adolf A. Berle Jr. and Gardner C. Means wrote a book entitled *The Modern Corporation and Private Property*. A critique of corporate management for being aloof and complacent, out of touch with the consumer and irresponsible to the stockholder, this volume became the bible of Marxists, left wing intellectuals and interventionist politicians. Under the banner of separation of ownership and control, the Berle-Means thesis led to an attack on the corporate structure from which today's top executives are still reeling.

With this background, one would have thought that the people urging a greater role for the public sector would have welcomed the advent of the corporate raider. For this new breed of capitalist has sent shivers down the spines of the denizens of the boardroom. Swooping down, launching "unfriendly" or "hostile" takeover bids, these corporate raiders have succeeded in replacing management from coast to coast in dozens of industries, and in frightening thousands of other out-of-touch chief executive officers into greater responsibility.

At least under the theory of "the enemy of my enemy is my friend," it might have been expected that critics of the marketplace, noticeably the followers of Berle and Means, would have rallied 'round the cause of the corporate raider.

In the event, however, this expectation has remained unfulfilled. Not only has the activity of the corporate raider been deprecated by the champions of government interference in the marketplace, but it has been roundly condemned by practically all pundits and commentators on public policy. In 1987, the left-leaning film director Oliver Stone distilled the common image of the corporate raider into the supposedly loathsome Gordon Gekko, brilliantly portrayed in an Oscar-winning performance by Michael Douglas. And this is the image of Gekko under which the corporate raider must labor in the present day.

Yet, despite this all-but-universal criticism, the unfriendly takeover bid has benefited consumers and stockholders, and served notice on complacent management across the board. In one celebrated case that unfolded shortly before Stone's film *Wall Street* was released, corporate guerrilla Carl Icahn put in a bid for a block of shares of Phillips Petroleum. Stung by Icahn's bid, Phillips' executives offered to improve a recapitalization plan they had been forced to put forth in response to an earlier planned takeover, this one by T. Boone Pickens. As a result, Icahn walked away with a cool $50 million, Pickens registered a profit of $89 million on a resale of his holdings to the company, all Phillips' shareholders gained from the better offer, and the oil firm itself was left far leaner and meaner than before.

Needless to say, neither Icahn nor Pickens nor any of the other masterminds of "the 1980s takeover boom," were publicly thanked for the good they had done. On the contrary: both men were not only mocked by Oliver Stone, they were also robbed of the opportunity to do any more such good by a rash of anti-takeover statutes adopted late in the decade. Henry Manne reported that hostile takeovers had "declined to four percent from fourteen percent of all mergers."

"MY GOD, LASKER HAS DONE IT! HE'S TAKEN OVER
HOMEX INDUSTRIES—THEY'VE TAKEN DOWN THE
'UNITED FUND' PENNANT AND HOISTED THE JOLLY ROGER!"

The conventional wisdom holds that this outcome is a good one for investors, but the facts show otherwise. No story of the corporate raider can ignore the role of the heroic Michael Milken. Assume there was a hotel worth $20 million as a present discounted capital value. Given an interest rate of 5%, this concern should throw off roughly $1 million to its owners. But stipulate that due to inefficiency, or general avarice, or to the fact that the CEO salary was far higher than justified, or a combination of all such phenomena, the owners were earning far less than that in dividends. And, guess what? The stock was trading at a lower value than might have prevailed, had these tape worm factors not been in operation.

Enter the "evil" Michael Milken. He swoops in, purchases enough of the stock in this corporation to kick out the old board and replace it with his own nominees. This is considered a "hostile" takeover by a corporate "raider." From whence springs the hostility? All Milken did was buy up a mess of stocks. Did he threaten any of these stock owners that they would walk the plank if they did not sell to him? No, of course not; we are talking arm's-length stock market deals here. We can logically infer that the owners of these stocks preferred the price offered them by the "raider," otherwise they would not have sold out. No, the "hostility," instead, stems from the CEO and his cronies who were mismanaging this hotel into the ground.

The Milkins of the world are akin to the canary in the mine; they are the Distant Early Warning Line for the economy. When they get active, it is in response to something rotten that is going on. And what was the public reaction to this corporate raider? Instead of hoisting him up on their shoulders and holding ticker tape parades in his honor, he was given the back of the public's hand to his face. To wit, he was prosecuted by the Securities and Exchange Commission for insider trading, violations of U.S. Securities Laws and other financial felonies. He pled guilty only after the authorities threatened to go after his ailing brother. For shame.

II. LABOR

6.

THE HATCHET MAN

In the movie "Up in the Air," George Clooney travels around the country firing people. He's what's known in the corporate world as a hatchet man. He does what the bosses at the endless stream of companies portrayed in the movie don't have the stomach for.

It seems unfair to all right-thinking progressives that an employee could be fired without "cause"; that a man's employment could be terminated for any reason deemed appropriate by his employer—or for no reason at all. And yet, this is precisely what traditional "at will" employment means. It seems unjust to most people to fire an employee without good cause. To some, advocates of guaranteed lifelong employment, it appears unfair to terminate employment for *any* cause, perhaps barring criminal or grossly immoral behavior.

The reason for the widespread popularity of this view is that most people view a job as a possession. We speak of "my job," and we implicitly assume property rights over the employment relation. If it is disrupted—whether by a firing, a plant closing or a "scab" taking away the job during a union dispute—many people feel as victimized as they would if they were the victims of a theft.

"OH NO YOU DON'T, MR. LOGGINS, GET BACK IN THE GODDAM STORE AND BUY THAT WASHING MACHINE YOU WERE ASKING ABOUT! YOU'RE MY CUSTOMER AND DON'T YOU EVER FORGET IT!"

But this analysis is faulty. A job merely describes a relationship between two parties. It is not something that can be owned by either of them, and certainly not something that is the rightful possession of only one. The possessive mode of the phrase "my job" is a highly unfortunate and misleading figure of speech.

There are other such possessive phrases in the English language, but they rarely create analogous mischief. We speak, for example, of "my wife," or "my husband," without assuming, in this modern era at least, that such people can be held to the relationship against their will. We speak of "my tailor" or "my butcher," without denoting any possessive quality. If the merchant in question picks up stakes and moves to another town or retires or shifts to a different occupation, we might regret the inconvenience, but scarcely feel our rights are violated. Obversely, the merchant may speak of "my customer," but he knows he has no proprietary rights thereby. If "his customer" goes elsewhere, for any reason, cause or whim, the merchant has no case against him. Nor is it even considered unfair.

In order to see firing without cause from a correct perspective, let us consider divorcing without cause. Most people of good will see our present no-fault divorce laws as a vast improvement over the old system. Previously, in order to divorce a spouse, one had to prove cruelty, or adultery, or some such. Nowadays, one can end a marriage for any or no reason. Would our friends on the liberal left want to push back the clock on divorce law? Hardly.

In like manner, for the employer who wishes to "divorce" his employee, there should be provision for no-fault divorce. That is to say, being fired without cause is not unfair or improper, no more than is being divorced without cause. If the one is a progressive step in human relations, then so is the other.

There is still another difficulty here. This view is asymmetric. Union members and their supporters complain bitterly over being *fired* without cause. But what about those who *quit* jobs without cause? If we took this perspective to its logical conclusion, leaving an employment slot without cause should be seen in the same negative regard. After all, the employer may be counting on the continued services of the worker, and in any case, it is "his" employee. Should *quitting* a job without proper cause be made illegal? No; of course not. The employee should be able to divorce his employer without a by-your-leave from anyone.

Of course, *both* are justified. Free men have the right to quit their jobs, and they also have the right to fire others—in the complete absence of cause. In the absence of a contract specifying otherwise, employer and employee should each be able to end their relationship whenever they want, for any reason, or for absolutely no reason.

Another important factor to consider in this context is the necessarily limited supply of job security. Who among us does not desire job security for himself, his friends, his neighbors, and his family?

And yet job security is in limited supply, and if some of us have more of it, such as union members and especially those who work in the public sector, then others of us will necessarily have less. True, job security for the entire community can be increased, but only at the cost of greater economic flexibility and retarded economic growth.

How does this work?

Consider an agrarian society of two or three centuries ago, before the onset of the industrial revolution. There were no changes. No innovations. No products suddenly imported from abroad. People were born, lived their lives and died doing things in much the same way for their whole time on Earth. They ate the same food, wore the same type of clothes, lived in the same style of housing and engaged in the same entertainment as in the days of yore.

Under such a system, as can readily be imagined, pretty much everyone in society had job security. With both bankruptcy and the creation of new firms practically unknown, there was much less reason to change jobs. Everything tended to be well-ordered, unchanging and *secure*.

But nowadays, we live in a time of continuous change. The horse and buggy industry gave way to the automobile. The Southeast Asians can now produce textiles more cheaply than North Americans—with the consequent loss of job security in North American textiles, and other such horse-and-buggy industries. Waiting in the wings are robots, ever more sophisticated computers, genetic engineering, and a whole host of other industries that only science fiction writers would have taken seriously just a few decades ago. All of these new ways of doing things will immeasurably improve our well-being. Indeed, the lives of billions of new human beings will come to depend upon them, in just the same way that those of most people now living on Earth would be impossible were it not for the mechanical and technical breakthroughs we now already enjoy.

But these new inventions will wreak havoc on present methods of production. If we are to adapt to this life-giving progress, job security will necessarily suffer. And if some of us are given enhanced job security, through special and privileged legislative enactment, the burden of adjustment to change will be unfairly shifted to the rest of us.

If people really want additional job security, in a way that poses no threat to the rest of society, let them pay for it themselves: either by accepting *lower* wages, or by taking out an insurance policy and paying premiums for the privilege of extra job security. So, let us give at least a cheer or two, and, maybe three, for the character played by George Clooney in the movie "Up in the Air."

7.

THE HOME-WORKER

A man's home may be his castle, but not as far as working there is concerned—at least, not according to those who advocate legislation restricting commercial activity in one's own domicile.

Originally, such laws were placed on the books in order to enforce earlier child labor and minimum wage laws. As well, unions protested vociferously that home-workers would be very difficult to organize, and the result would be a return to sweatshop conditions.

In the modern era, however, the people who wish to work at home are more likely to be professionals, managers, and sales representatives who can work independently and/or don't want to commute. Some may be women who are reasonably well-off and just wish to earn some extra money. For example, there was a flap a little while back over several hundred women in the New England states who were knitting snow mittens and ski caps and who justified this practice on the grounds of "freedom of enterprise." And, as if in order to show that not only politics makes strange bedfellows, they also defended themselves on the basis of women's liberation: being able to

"LOOK AT THAT POOR LADY, LEO! THEY OUGHTA
BAN THIS HOME KNITTING STUFF. THEY'RE WORSE
THAN THE OLD SWEATSHOPS!"

work at home was the only way that many of them could work
at all—while continuing to watch over their children.

But the debate over home knitters was really only a tempest
in a teapot. At most, it involved several thousand seamstresses
in an industry that had been on the verge of being supplanted
by technology for many years. Of far greater statistical signifi-
cance is the emerging trend toward the transplantation of clerical workers from offices to their homes. This has been made
possible on a significant scale by technological breakthroughs
in computer engineering, but if present trends continue, it is
possible that this small stream will turn into a tidal wave.

If this occurs, the union argument that cottage industry is
synonymous with sweatshop conditions will be given even
wider denigration. It is thus appropriate that we subject this

contention to critical analysis. For it is incorrect, and public policy based upon its supposed truth will, as a result, be counterproductive.

To begin with, we must admit that there is a certain superficial attractiveness to this view. After all, in the seventeenth and eighteenth centuries, when home work was the order of the day, economic conditions were indeed deplorable. But to argue that because A (cottage industry) and B (poverty) were both found at the same time in history, therefore A *caused* B, is to commit the fallacy known as *post hoc ergo propter hoc*. It makes as much or as little sense to claim that because the wheel existed long ago that this magnificent discovery actually caused a retrogression of civilization.

In actual point of fact, the organization of labor into gigantic bargaining units cannot at all account for increased standards of living. First of all, economic improvement has been occurring for hundreds of years, and while unions were formed as early as the late nineteenth century, they had no real power until the beginning of the twentieth. Secondly, there are numerous countries around the world, especially in the Orient, which have undergone "economic miracles," where unions are weak or non-existent. And thirdly, organized labor cannot take credit for an end to sweatshop conditions even in nations where it is well entrenched. This is because, alongside the gains that have undoubtedly been made in unionized industries, equal or greater benefits have been given to employees in the non-unionized sector, in such fields as computers, banking, and even domestic service.

If we can no longer countenance the idea that unionization is all that stands between the laborer and the sweatshop, then there is simply no case for interfering with the institution of home work, no matter how big it becomes. Moreover, it is silly to even entertain the notion that home-working is a step backward toward the sweat shop conditions of a bygone era. If it were, why would these people embrace it? From the fact that they voluntarily decide upon this step, we may logically infer that, at least in their own eyes, it *betters* their condition. If it didn't, they never would have embarked upon this type of economic activity.

And there is every reason for allowing this new form of industrial organization. People have a natural right to do whatever they please, provided only that their actions do not infringe on the rights of others to do exactly the same. Those who favor both unionism and women's liberation will have to make a choice: one or the other. As this example shows, they cannot have it both ways.

8.

PICKET-LINE CROSSER

There is no such thing as a "right to unionize." The claim that unionization is akin, or worse, an implication of the libertarian right to freely associate is entirely bogus. True, a labor organization *could* limit itself to organizing a mass quit unless and until they got what they wanted. That would indeed be compatible with the libertarian law of free association.

But *every* union with which I am familiar reserves the right to employ violence (that is, to *initiate* violence) against competing workers, e.g., scabs, whether in a "blue collar way" by beating them up, or in a "white collar way" by getting laws passed compelling employers to deal with them, and not with the scabs. (I once thought I had found an exception in the Christian Labor Association of Canada. But based on a telephone interview with a representative, I can say that while they eschew "blue collar" aggression, they support the "white collar" version.)

But what of the fact that there are many real life unions that have not actually engaged in the initiation of violence? Moreover, there are even people associated for many years with organized labor who have never witnessed the outbreak of actual physical aggression.

"YOUR HONOR, I CAUGHT THIS MAN TRYING TO STEAL THE JOB OF A STRIKING WORKER. ADDITIONALLY, DURING A BASEBALL GAME, WHILE 46 STRIKING WORKERS WERE UP AT BAT, THIS MAN ATTEMPTED TO DISRUPT IT !"

Let me clarify my position. My opposition is not merely to violence, but also to the threat of violence. Often, no actual force is needed, if the threat is serious enough, which, I contend it is under unionism as practiced in the U.S., Canada, and Western Europe.

Probably no member of the IRS ever engaged in the actual use of physical violence. This is because employees of this organization rely on the judicial and law enforcement arms of the U.S. government, which have overwhelming power (if not against the Iraqis, the Afghans nor the Iranians, then at least against their own citizenry). But it would be superficial to contend that the IRS does not engage in violence, or the threat of violence. This holds true also for the state trooper who gives you a traffic ticket. They are, and are trained to be, exceedingly polite. Yet, violence, or the threat of violence permeates their entire relationship with you.

I do not deny that sometimes management also engages in violence, or the threat of violence. My only contention is that it is possible to point to numerous cases where they do *not*, while the same is impossible for organized labor, at least in the countries I am discussing.

Further, the firm is always and necessarily so, in a defensive position vis-à-vis the union. If the latter would limit itself to mass quits, there would be very little reason for the company to initiate force against them. It would make far more sense for them to ignore the threat of organized labor and get on about the business of hiring replacement workers.

The threat emanating from unions is objective, not subjective. It is the threat, in the old blue collar days, that any competing worker, a "scab," would be beat up if he tried to cross a picket line, and, in the modern white collar era, that any employer who fires a striking union member and substitutes a replacement worker as a permanent hire, will be found in violation of various labor laws. (Why is it not "discriminatory" and "hateful," to describe workers willing to take less pay and compete with unionized labor as "scabs"? Should not this be considered on a par with using the "N" word for blacks, or the "K" word for Jews?)

Suppose a scrawny hold-up man confronts a burly football-player-type guy and demands his money, threatening that if the big guy does not give it up, the little guy will kick his butt. This is an objective threat, and it does not matter if the big guy laughs himself silly in reaction. Second scenario is the same as the first, only this time the little guy whips out a pistol and threatens to shoot the big guy unless he hands over his money.

Now, there are two kinds of big guys. One will feel threatened and give up his wallet. The second will attack the little guy (in self-defense, of course). Perhaps he is feeling omnipotent.

Perhaps he is wearing a bullet-proof vest. It does not matter. The threat is a threat, regardless of the reaction of the big guy, regardless of his inner psychological response.

Now, let us return to labor-management relations. The union objectively threatens scabs and employers who hire them. This is *necessitated*, purely as a matter of law. It is a fact, not based on psychological feelings on anyone's part. In contrast, while it cannot be denied that sometimes employers initiate violence against workers, they need not *necessarily* do it. Often, however, they do not employ violence at all; in contrast, given union inspired labor laws, unions are *continually* violating the rights of employers. Sometimes, employers utilize violence against organized labor, but in self-defense. For example, when they defend their property, or "scabs," against strikers.

We must never succumb to the siren song of union thuggery. Let us now consider eight objections to the foregoing.

1. LEGITIMATE UNIONISM?

Theoretically, unions are compatible with a free society. Yes. Nothing said above should be taken to be inconsistent with this view. All such a union would have to do is to eschew both white and blue-collar crime. I only argue that it has never happened, not that it would be impossible for it to occur.

However, surely a worker's association that totally eschews the initiation of violence, or even the threat thereof, deserves different nomenclature from organizations it only superficially resembles; e.g., unions. My suggestion is that we not characterize as a union any labor organization that strictly limits itself to the threat of quitting en masse.

What then should we call a group of workers who eschew both beating up scabs and laws compelling employers to bargain with them? Here are some possibilities: workers' associations, employee groups, organizations of staff members, etc. Thus, are workers' associations as defined above compatible with free enterprise? You bet your boots they are. Do unions or organized labor as they presently operate qualify in this regard? No, a thousand times no.

2. PUBLIC SECTOR UNIONS

What is their status? Public sector unions present theoretical libertarianism with a very complex challenge, albeit in a slightly different manner than do private sector unions. In this case, they are not necessarily incompatible with the free society, but, as it happens, there are no actual cases in existence of such employee organizations that *are* consistent with economic freedom.

The complexity presented by public sector unions is that, on the one hand, from a libertarian perspective they can be seen as a counterweight to illegitimate governments, while on the other hand they constitute an attack on innocent citizens. Each of these different roles calls for a somewhat different analysis.

Let us start with the first case. For the limited-government libertarian, or minarchist, the state is illegitimate if, and to the extent it exceeds its proper bounds. These, typically, include armies (for *defense* against foreign powers, not *offense* against them), police to keep local criminals in check (that is, rapists, child exploiters, and murderers, etc., not victimless "criminals" such as drug dealers, prostitutes, etc.), and courts to determine guilt or innocence. Some more moderate advocates of laissez faire add to this list agencies to build and maintain roads, treat and track communicable diseases and provide inoculations, fire protection, and mosquito control. For the anarcho-libertarian, of course, there is no such thing as a licit government.

What, then, are libertarians to say about a public sector teachers' union on strike against a state school? (A similar analysis holds for public sector unions in garbage collection, postal service, transit, or any other industry where government involvement is improper in the first place.) The correct analysis

"... I DON'T THINK YOU'RE GOING TO GET A FAIR SHAKE <u>HERE</u>, J.B. ."

of this situation is, "A plague on both your houses." For not one, but *both* of these organizations are illegitimate. There is no libertarian who can favor government schools, whether anarchist or minarchist. (Milton Friedman, who champions public schools as long as they operate under a voucher system, thus falls outside the realm of libertarianism on this question.) So, from a libertarian perspective both sides of this dispute are illegitimate. There are two contending forces, *both* of them in the wrong. From a *strategic* point of view, we may well even support the union vis-à-vis the government, since they are the weaker of our two opponents. But from a principled perspective, we must look upon the two of them as all men of good will would witness a battle between the Bloods and the Crips, or between Nazi Germany and Communist U.S.S.R. Root for both of them!

Now let us consider the second case. Here, we note that the public sector union does much more than attack illegitimate government. It also vastly inconveniences the populace. When schools are closed, garbage is not collected, the buses do not run—because public sector unions utilize violence and the threat thereof to these ends—then the libertarian response is clear: total opposition to the offending unions.

Let us take one last crack at public sector unions, which brings about a further complication. Consider an episode of the ABC news program 20/20 about how public-employee unions are fighting against people who volunteer for the public good, specifically, the "Give Me a Break" segment by host John Stossel. (See "No Good Deed Goes Unpunished: Are Volunteers Taking Workers' Jobs?" at ABCNEWS.com.)

The general issue is that citizens have been volunteering to do things like help public sector unionists collect trash in parks, aid them in planting flowers, help them stack books in public libraries, etc., and the unions have reacted viciously, as is their custom.

Before we can shed libertarian light on this contentious issue, let us first ask: What is the libertarian analysis of ordinary people volunteering to help the government do jobs it should not be doing in the first place? To put it in this way is almost to answer the question.

There is no difference in principle between volunteering to help the state perform illegitimate acts (of course, these are not illicit *per se*, as are the concentration camps; rather, it is improper, in libertarian theory, for *governments* to take on such responsibilities) such as operating and maintaining libraries, schools, parks, etc., and sending them monetary donations for such purposes. In either case, one is aiding and abetting evil, and risking being found guilty of crimes against humanity by a future libertarian Nuremberg trial court.

Repeat after me: free enterprise, good, (excessive, for the minarchists) government, bad. Once again, from the top: *free enterprise, good, (excessive) government, bad!* The appellation,

"JOSEPH, PULL INTO THE BREAKDOWN LANE,
STOP THE CAR, GET OUT AND REACH INTO
WHERE I'M SITTING AND PINCH ME SO I CAN
FIND OUT IF I'M DREAMING."

"libertarian," is an honorific. It is too precious to be bestowed on all those who falsely claim it. People who support (excessive) government are simply not entitled to its use, at least in the specific context in which they violate the non-aggression axiom. Thus, John Stossel is indeed a libertarian on many other issues, but certainly not on this one.

Here is a lesson for libertarians: if you want to be worthy of this designation, and desire to contribute money to a good cause, do not give to a government that goes beyond its legitimate authority. There are many worthy causes that *oppose* statist depredations, not *support* them. If you want to be worthy of this honorific and wish to donate time to a good cause, e.g., by collecting garbage, planting flowers, or filing books, etc., then do so for the relevant *private* groups, whether charitable or profit-seeking, it matters not one whit.

3. LIBERTARIANS JOIN A UNION?

Is it proper, if it is even logically possible, for a libertarian to join a coercive union? Much as I hate to be controversial (Okay, okay, I don't mind it a bit), my answer is yes. There are many issues upon which I disagreed with William F. Buckley, but his decision to join ACTRA, the Alliance of Canadian Cinema, Television and Radio Artists, is not one of them. (This was the requirement imposed upon him for being allowed to air his television show, *Firing Line*.)

Why would I take such a seemingly perverted stance? Let me answer by indirection. Given that it is illegitimate for the government to run schools and universities, is it illegitimate for a libertarian to join them whether as a student or a professor? Given that it is illegitimate for the government to organize a post office, is it illegitimate for a libertarian to mail a letter? Given that it is illegitimate for the government to build and manage roads, streets, and sidewalks, is it illegitimate for a libertarian to utilize these amenities? Given that it is illegitimate for the government to provide currency (the Constitution allows this, but for the libertarian, only the market may properly do so), is it illegitimate for a libertarian to utilize dollar bills?

True confession time. I have been a student of public schools: grade school, high school, and college. I have even been a professor at several public colleges and universities. I regularly purchase stamps from the evil government post office, and have the audacity to mail letters. I walk on public sidewalks and avail myself of streets and highways. I have U.S. fiat currency in my wallet. Mea culpa? Not at all.

If Ayn Rand's heroic character Ragnar Danneskjöld has taught us anything, it is that the government is not the legitimate owner of what it claims. Why, then, should we respect its "private property rights" when there is no just reason to do so? If this means that libertarians can partake of services for which they favor privatization, then so be it.

It is similar with coercive unions. If a hold-up man demands your money at the point of a gun, giving it up is *not* incompatible with libertarianism, even though it amounts to acquiescing in theft. If organized labor threatens you with bodily harm unless you join with it and pay dues to it, agreeing to do so does not remove the victim from the ranks of libertarianism. Buckley, to give him credit, never ceased inveighing against the injustice done to him in this way. If he had reversed field and starting *defending* unions, then even what little claim he had as a libertarian would have vanished. In this regard, there is all the world of difference between a Marxist professor at a public university who promotes interventionism, and a libertarian who opposes it.

4. Not aware of violence

Many members are simply not aware of any violence in their own unions. But, many employees of the IRS are probably not aware that what they are doing amounts to the threat of the initiation of violence. All union members should hardly necessarily be aware of this for the thesis of this chapter to be correct. After the British left India, the government of the latter began polling people in far removed rural villages as to their thoughts on this matter; they had to stop when they learned that the villagers were not aware that the British had been there in the first place. Heck, there are probably some people out there who still think the Earth is flat, or that socialism is an ethical and efficacious system! That does not make it so.

5. Self-defense

We now consider the objection that union violence did indeed exist, but was justified on the grounds that this was only in self-defense, against employers, scabs, or foreigners. Let us consider each of these in turn.

Yes, employers are violent too. The Pinkertons spring immediately to mind. Some of these cases were justified in self-defense, against prior union aggression, some were not. In the former case, there is certainly no warrant for invasive behavior on the part of organized labor. But even the latter cases cannot serve as justification for pervasive union aggression. At best, this can validate self-defense on the part of the rank and file in those cases of employer aggression only.

And what of "scabs?" The claim, here, is that "scabs" are stealing, or, better yet, attempting to steal, union jobs. But the scab can only "steal" a job if it is *owned*, like a coat or a car. However, a job is very different. It is *not* something anyone can own. Rather, a job is an *agreement* between two parties, employer and employee. But when an employer is trying to hire a scab and fire the unionist, this shows, at the very least, he no longer *agrees*. Do not be fooled by the expression "my job." It does not denote ownership, any more than "my wife," "my husband," "my friend," "my customer," or "my tailor" indicates possession in any of those contexts. Rather, all of these phrases are indicative of voluntary interaction, and end (apart from marriage laws which may prohibit this) when the agreement ceases.

Then, there is the supposed "threat" imposed by Mexican workers (or Indian or Japanese workers, whoever is the economic scapegoat of the day). Remember that "giant sucking sound?" The best remedy for this bit of economic illiteracy is to read up on the case for free trade (see the chapter on the smuggler in this book).

6. BUT THEY SIGNED A CONTRACT

Since the employer signed a labor contract, he should be forced to abide by its provisions. But why should the employer have to honor a contract that was signed under duress? There can be no such thing as a purely volitional contract between

"OLD J. B. WOULD BE ECSTATIC IF HE KNEW HE WENT TO HIS FINAL REWARD CROSSING A PICKET LINE....."

the firm and a union, with the sword of Damocles hanging over the former. Suppose I held a gun on you, threatened to shoot you unless you signed a "contract" with me, promising to give me $100 per week. Later on, when you were safe, you reneged on this "contract." Certainly, you would be within your rights.

7. MAXIMIZE INCOME

Unions maximize income for their members. Therefore, they are justified.

First of all, even if this were true, any criminal could say no less. A hold-up man, too, wants to maximize his return and does so by committing aggression against non-aggressors. How is the unionist any different than the hold-up man in this regard?

Secondly, it is by no means clear that organized labor is the last best chance for economic well-being on the part of the working man. Anyone ever heard of the rust belt? Unions located in places stretching from Illinois to Massachusetts demanded wages and fringe benefits in excess of productivity levels, and employers were powerless to resist. The result was "runaway shops." Either they ran into bankruptcy, or they relocated to places like Alabama, Mississippi, and Louisiana, where unionism was seen more for the economic and moral scourge that it is, than in Taxachussetts. If organizing workers into unions is the "be all and end all" of prosperity, how is it that wages and working conditions are very good in computers, insurance, banking, and a plethora of other non-unionized industries? How is it that real wages were rising before the first advent of such labor organizations at the turn of the twentieth century? How is it that at the end of the twentieth century, union membership was falling, while wages were increasing?

8. Hierarchy, the real problem.

The real problem with unions is that they are hierarchical; the libertarian must oppose *all* hierarchical organizations, which certainly includes employers, too.

But this is just plain silly. Libertarians oppose the initiation of coercion or the threat thereof, not hierarchy. Yes, all groups that violate the non-aggression axiom of libertarians are hierarchical. Governments, gangs, rapists, impose their will, by force, on their victims. They give orders. And yes, in all hierarchies, people at the top of the food chain give orders to those below them. But the difference, and this is crucial, between illicit and licit hierarchy is that the recipients of orders

"...LISTEN, LOUIE, YOU STARTED OFF JUST LOANSHARKIN', AND NOW THE BOSS HEARS YOU'RE DOIN' SOME 'SELF-DEALIN', AND HE DON'T LIKE IT..."

in the latter case have *agreed* to accept them, but this does not at all apply in the former case.

When the rapist orders the victim to carry out his commands, this is *illegitimate* hierarchy. When the conductor orders the cellist to do so, this is an aspect of *legitimate* hierarchy. I oppose unions not because they are hierarchical, but because their victim-scabs have never agreed to carry out their orders.

9.

THE DAYCARE PROVIDER

Daycare for profit? In the minds of some, the very concept boggles the imagination.

According to these people, on the one hand we have the nation's children—tender, sweet, cuddly, cute, and lovable. On the other hand we have the evil profit system, hard-hearted, cold, and calculating at best, with a cash register for a soul.

Are we to deliver our little kiddies to the "tender mercies of the profit-mongering capitalist system?" Not if the usual socialist suspects have anything to say about it. In their view, when money becomes the first consideration, quality takes a poor second. You can do that with a product, but not with children. Children are the major resource of the future.

But this dichotomy between money and quality, between profits and care, is a sheer fabrication. First of all, there have been numerous cases throughout recorded history of faithful rendition of service—for money! Examples from the health field include doctors, psychiatrists, psychologists, and nurses. But members of *every* profession, mechanics and babysitters, plumbers and even economists, both provide and charge for their services.

Secondly, the argument completely misconstrues the role of profits in our society. Far from being an impediment to high quality service, profits are almost always a spur to exemplary conduct and evidence of its existence. It is no coincidence that companies which are practically synonymous with high profits are also well known for providing reliable products and service. It is rather a *lack* of profits that is correlated with failure to provide the public with a good or service deemed more valuable than its cost. How else could it be? Do we really expect low profits to be linked with exemplary service or high profits with unsatisfied customers? (I am now ignoring firms that earn profits not through market transactions, but, rather, on the basis of government largesse: subsidies, special privileges, tariff protections, etc.)

In any case, whether private or public, daycare cannot be contrived without the intermediation of the monetary nexus. In the private system, parents can contract on a voluntary basis with the childcare workers of their choice, or they can form cooperatives based on voluntary donations. But with public daycare, funds would be forcibly taken from all citizens via taxes, whether or not they were interested in this service or even had children.

Advocates of nationalized daycare would have us believe that they are disinterested parties, concerned only with the welfare of the children. Such, however, is hardly the case. They are rather an organized economic pressure group, who aim to maximize their own incomes in competition with alternative suppliers of the service: namely nannies, babysitters, daycare purveyors who work at home (often with children of their own), as well as with, dare I say it, private, commercial daycare concerns.

The proponents of the "Big Brother—let government do it" school of thought have already succeeded in setting up arbitrary and discriminatory rules which discourage private daycare alternatives. For example, in some jurisdictions, a private daycare company must pay $150 for a development permit issued by the municipality—while a nonprofit center, registered as a society, need pay only one dollar! Moreover, private firms must invest their own money in the endeavor, while nonprofit centers may receive government grants (paid for, of course, out of tax revenues received from private enterprise). And then there are the limitations on the number of children each center is allowed to serve, and the staff-hiring restrictions, which impose a discriminatory and irrelevant "credentialism" on private daycare owners. It is easy to see how these requirements serve the professional-oriented daycare service association, but not the parents of the children enrolled in private daycare. These restrictions also violate the rights of the qualified personnel who might staff such institutions—without benefit of the sometimes artificial and needless advanced university degrees in child care.

Some governments threaten to do worse than this. There are plans, even, to take away tax concessions from married women staying at home, and use the proceeds to increase deductions for money spent on outside daycare. The state, in other words, would take money away from those women who care for their children at home, and give it to mothers who use daycare facilities. What possible justification could there be for government giving families financial incentives to increase the number of hours per week that children are cared for outside the home?

In looking for explanations, one must not be paranoid. On the other hand, it would not do to overlook any explanation out of fear of appearing alarmist.

So let us consider one possible explanation: that the institutions of the centralizing, interventionist state and that of the family have historically been at odds with one another, and that this present threat is but another chapter in this unfolding saga.

A government bent on taking an ever larger role in the life of its citizenry sooner or later runs into conflict with other institutions—churches, voluntary clubs, the family—which

"...ME? WELL, I RAN A FOR-PROFIT DAYCARE FACILITY, AND A STATE INSPECTOR SAID THAT OUR NURSERY RHYMES WERE RACIST, SEXIST AND FOSTERED ANTIPATHY TOWARD THE PEOPLE OF THE 3RD WORLD. THEY CLOSED ME UP AND GAVE ME 5 YEARS."

also command the strong loyalty of the people. And when this occurs, the government must either give up its totalitarian aspirations, or determine to enter a give-no-quarter war with these alternative institutions.

In the countries that languished behind the Iron Curtain, the war was fought long ago, and institutions such as churches, clubs, the family, and the ethnic group were long ago vanquished.

In North America, the battle is yet to be fought in its entirety. That is to say, there is still hope for private institutions such as the family.

But every time the government successfully promotes daycare above the natural level that would otherwise ensue, or artificially entices women out of the home and into the workforce, or attacks the tax treatment of married women living at home in favor of those who give up their children to the tender mercies of the state, to that extent it weakens the family as an alternative to government.

The logical extension of such a procedure would be family life as it has been lived for generations in Central and Eastern Europe—a less viable institution than we have been able to maintain at home—so far.

In order to preserve and protect the North American family, it is not necessary to take a "maximalist" position: that the government should do everything in its power to artificially strengthen the family, by penalizing alternative institutions such as unmarried status or childlessness. To do this smacks of putting the fox in charge of the chicken coop.

It is enough to adopt a "minimalist" position: that the state merely refrains from adopting policies which lead to family disruption. That is what "laissez faire" is all about.

This chapter is dedicated to all those dedicated childcare providers who were jailed by governmental authorities on trumped-up charges.

10.

THE AUTOMATOR

I t's called many things—artificial intelligence, the microdot
electronic revolution, the Age of Robotics.

Whatever the name, it can perform numerous and
amazing tasks. Modern computers, coupled with silicon chip-
based integrated circuits, can now diagnose lung diseases,
locate mineral deposits, play chess at better than a grand
master level, cut logs, assemble autos, and do other industrial
tasks far more efficiently than human beings.

These electronic servants, moreover, work twenty-four
hours a day, seven days a week, fifty-two weeks a year, with
no time off for coffee breaks, holidays or gossip. They never
call in sick or talk back to the boss (unless programmed to do
so); nor do they file legal grievances against their employers.

Wondrous and marvelous as these accomplishments are,
there is, according to some, quite a large worm in the apple.
The complaints are numerous:

• Millions of clerical, sales, and service workers—in banking,
insurance, and general business offices—have lost their jobs to
automatic word processors and related office automation.

• When a steel corporation opens a fully automated plant,
it can produce the same amount of output with fifty percent of
the workers used in an older type of operation.

• New robots will take more of the places of humans on automobile assembly lines; the Japanese are the worst offenders in this regard; they are already up to a fifth generation of such artificially intelligent machines.

• There have been widespread claims that the new automation has increased the degree of anomie suffered by the human beings who work alongside it. Complaints include failing morale, depersonalization, and alienation from the workplace.

Based on these and other horror stories, a reaction to the new generation of computers has set in. In addition to growth restrictions, there is a threatened technological moratorium in the offing. Worse, a new generation of Luddites (the original Luddites were the people in the eighteenth century who burned newly invented knitting looms out of fear for their jobs) stands ready to fight the artificially intelligent computers—with sabotage.

Given this specter, a more measured response would appear to be indicated. We must realize that as long as there are unmet needs and people willing to work to attain these ends, there will be new positions created. From the vantage point of our agricultural economy of 200 years ago, it would have been impossible to predict precisely what kinds of jobs would come into existence today. In like manner, we cannot now predict which occupations will arise to take the place of those shown to be unnecessary by the new computer revolution.

However, we know that they *will* be created, and we know why. If a robot, at both minimal outlay and subsequent maintenance cost, is really able to replace a thousand workers (to take the "worst" possible scenario), then some truly monumental results will ensue, and each of them will create new employment opportunities.

In the first instance, immense profits will be earned by such companies. Their shareholders (and/or private owners) will either spend or save their newfound wealth. Spending will boost other industry, while saving will drive down interest

rates (naturally, that is; not by the central planning Federal Reserve), creating new loan opportunities and new employment.

But such profit levels cannot long endure. In a reasonably free market system, new entrants will swarm in, to take advantage of the greater than ordinary returns. By purchasing additional robotic factors of production (and hence raising their prices), and by selling more such products at lower prices, profit levels will soon be dissipated. The former will encourage more employment in robot production, and the latter will enable consumers to purchase yet even more with a given dollar, thus again raising their standard of living. This will lead to still more employment in those areas where the new purchasing power is spent.

It was through a process such as this that large employment shifts took place in the past, amid the same hysterical worry. There is no doubt that it will continue to work in the same way. It was once feared that automatic spinning mills would permanently unemploy the entire hand-weaving industry. Instead, the results were cheaper clothing and more jobs in cloth making. First-generation computers were supposed to create a permanent "army of the unemployed" among office workers. Instead, companies like IBM, Microsoft, Google, and Yahoo have created millions of jobs throughout the economy, with lower prices and higher standards of living to boot.

No less will be true of the new artificial intelligence revolution. The worm in the apple will not be a cold, faceless computer-robot, taking the bread away from the workers' tables. Instead it will be modern Luddites who once again threaten progress.

The Luddites are continually engaging in destruction, hooliganism, and vandalism against any and all introductions of automatic equipment, ranging from automated shuttles at airports to Light Rapid Transit that runs without benefit of (live) conductors on board. Part of this is motivated by the fact that these machines cannot join unions. But a greater part of these nefarious activities is engendered by peoples' fear that this machinery will supplant human effort. After all, goes their "reasoning," if robots do the work, what will remain for people to do?

The original Luddite, one Ned Ludd, went on the first such Luddite rampage, burning knitting looms because they enabled one person to do the work of twenty. Lud was entirely well-intentioned. Who, after all, wants to see nineteen people unemployed, even if the twentieth can thereby increase his productivity to match the entire group working with inferior technology? This would be no less than a tragedy—economically, morally, spiritually, and socially.

In like manner, the philosophy underlying more modern vandalism may well have been benevolent in origin, even if its methods left something to be desired. Those behind the destruction may have feared that unemployment rates would rise, at least compared to the situation in which each train or shuttle had a human driver. In this view, these machines had supplanted several hundred job slots, the number of train engineers who might otherwise have been used.

But a moment's reflection will convince us that an automated system has not lost us these jobs, nor any other jobs. First of all, additional employees, skilled at computer technology, were needed to construct the equipment at the outset. Secondly, there are the salaries for human motormen that will not be paid. These monies can be used instead for other purposes: for creating still more "robots," in order to accomplish new and additional tasks which would have been impossible to finance, or for extra consumption of already existing goods. Whichever of these options is chosen, it will mean increased employment in these other fields.

But the core myth here is the assumption that there is only so much work to be done in the world. Sometimes called the "lump of labor" fallacy, this economic view holds that the people of the world only require a limited amount of labor on their behalf. When this amount is surpassed, there will be no more work to be done, and hence, there will be no more jobs for the workers. In this perspective, making sure that automatic equipment is not employed is of overriding importance. For if these machines do too much, they will ruin things for everyone; there will be exactly that amount no longer available for people to do. By "hogging up" the limited amount of work which exists, they leave too little for human beings. It is as if the amount of work that can be done resembles a pie of a fixed size. If robots are allowed to seize some of it, we Homo sapiens will have to make do with less.

If this economic view of the world were correct, there might indeed be something to be said for the philosophy of vandalism. At least, there would be some justification for insisting that automatic machines not be put into operation.

However, there is as much work to be done as there are unfulfilled desires. Since human wants are, for all practical purposes, limitless, the amount of work to be done is also without end. Therefore, no matter how much work the robot completes, it cannot possibly exhaust or even make any kind of dent in the amount of work to be done, let alone an appreciable one.

If it does not "take work away from people" (because there is a limitless amount of work to be done), what effect *does* computer technology have? It increases production. Because of the efforts of the robots, the size of the pie increases—the pie that will then be shared among all those human beings who took part in its production or who benefit from its use.

Consider in this regard the plight of a family shipwrecked in the tropics. When the Swiss Family Robinson sought refuge on an island, their store of belongings consisted only of what was salvaged from the ship. The meager supply of capital goods, plus their own laboring ability, determined whether—and how well—they survived. Any Swiss Family Robinson faces an unending list of desires, while the means at their disposal for the satisfaction of these desires is extremely limited.

If we suppose that all the members of the family set to work with the material resources at their disposal, we will find that they can satisfy only some of their desires.

What would be the effect of having a robot at their disposal in such a situation? Suppose that, with the aid of technology, the family becomes able to produce twice as much per day as before. Will this be the ruination of the family? Will it "take work away" from the other family members, and wreak havoc upon the mini-society they have created?

It is obvious that this will not be the outcome. On the contrary, the machinery will be seen as the benefit it is, since there is no danger that the increased productivity it brings about will cause the family to run out of work to do.

If the new technology can produce ten extra units of transportation services, it may become possible for other members of the family to be relieved of such chores. New jobs will be assigned to them. Clearly, the end result will be greater satisfaction for the family. In like manner, because of robotics, society as a whole will move toward greater satisfaction and prosperity.

Thus the reasoning underlying the philosophy of vandalism is flawed. There are indeed problems with a government initiative which utilizes automation for mass transit, but the lack of human motormen is not one of them.

Still, the vandals who damage modern machinery are far from alone in their thinking. I recently looked down at my morning newspaper and saw a headline in bold black letters: "Women Battle Robots." "What's this?" I said to myself. "Have robots landed from outer space, and are they attacking our womenfolk?" Greatly concerned, I turned to read the newspaper account. I am happy to report that all the brouhaha was just a false alarm. No extra-terrestrial robots had been burning, pillaging, and raping. Rather, the newspaper story was about the introduction of new fish-cleaning machinery by a local fish processing company. The union was vociferously protesting the introduction of new automated equipment. And since most of the fish washers in the union are women, this accounted for the rather hysterical headline.

At first glance, these unionized women seem to have had a case. After all, many of their jobs were being made obsolete by robots that can clean fish faster and more cheaply than they. But, of course, there were benefits as well, although these particular women only participated in them in their role as consumers. With lower costs in the industry, the savings will either lead to greater profits or be passed on to the ultimate buyers of fish in the form of decreased prices. But extra profits mean more jobs—as this money will tend to be invested—and decreased prices will encourage consumers to buy more fish, also potentially creating additional employment.

As a matter of fact, the union undoubtedly owes many of its *present* jobs to *past* introductions of more efficient technology. After all, if fish were still caught by dangling a worm at the end of a string off the end of a dock, there would be precious few jobs in the fish processing industry—and precious little fish to feed the world's hungry populations.

But science-fiction writer Isaac Asimov saw the truth half a century ago, in the famous *I, Robot* stories which have recently been adapted to film: robots are a blessing to humankind, not a menace. If politicians really have the interests of the consuming public in mind, they will adopt a *laissez-faire* policy in this matter.

III. MEDICAL

11.

THE SMOKER

Cigarette smokers are now an endangered species. No-smoking zones have been established in hospitals, office buildings, recreational centers, shopping malls, and other places of congregation all over the United States. Cities and municipalities coast to coast have amended their health by laws so as to further proscribe the limits within which smoking is still allowed. In many cases, outright bans have been imposed. For example, cigarette smoking has been prohibited entirely in bars as well as all restaurants, in both San Francisco and New York. Tobacco advertising has long been severely limited, and there are now calls from otherwise respectable quarters for its outright elimination. There is little doubt that at this rate, government will soon prohibit smoking altogether on a nationwide basis, indoors and out.

The reason for this spate of activity is not hard to discern. Smoking has long been regarded as harmful to those who indulge in it. Moreover, recent medical evidence appears to suggest that non-smokers who inhabit the same enclosed rooms as smokers are also endangered, by the secondary effects of this practice. It may be rather hypocritical for a government which still subsidizes tobacco growers to climb onto the anti-smoking

bandwagon, and even attempt to lead the parade, but in the furor to wipe out this "vile" habit, logical consistency has been one of the first victims.

There are basically two ways to address the issue of smoking. One is by government fiat, and the second is by allowing the institutions of the free enterprise system to deal with the problem. Unfortunately, the political leaders of our society are so philosophically accustomed to use legislation as a bludgeon for all difficulties that the second type of solution has never even been publicly contemplated. Indeed, it is no exaggeration to say that most people have never even heard of it. How, then, would the market deal with the challenge of tobacco use?

Although it is always risky to try to anticipate the workings of a free marketplace, one scenario would have each business firm deciding for itself whether or not to impose a smoking ban, and if so, of what type. Some might allow smoking in all

areas at all times. Others might set aside special zones, which might vary with the time of day or the day of the week. Still others might be tempted to deal with the problem in ways that are not yet known.

Given this panoply of different smoking rules at different establishments, customers would then sort themselves out accordingly. They would patronize those which pleased them most. Firms would now compete with one another, not only with regard to their primary good or service (restaurant, department store, etc.) but also as pertains to the smoking rules they had set up.

And the same analysis applies to the workplace. There would be an "invisible hand" in operation here too, guiding employers to set up the smoking rules which would best suit their respective employees. How would this work? Let us suppose that a given industry is composed of people who are avid anti-smokers (for example, producers of health food products). Allowing this practice to take place on the factory premises, even in small and strictly limited areas, would thus be for them a strong negative non-pecuniary effect; it would be equivalent to imposing upon them any other undesirable working condition. In such a case, the workers would be more likely than otherwise to quit and take jobs elsewhere. They would only maintain their former high attachment to their present employer if compensated for this—by higher pecuniary wages. In such circumstances, it would clearly be in the interest of the firm to prohibit smoking throughout the premises.

Now, consider a business concern which employs people who are quite oblivious to the dangers of smoking (rodeo cowboys might be an example). A ban on the practice in this case would be viewed as an undesirable working condition, just the opposite of its interpretation in the previous example. Here, the forces of the market would work in the direction of allowing the widest range for smoking. Otherwise, the employees would be attracted elsewhere, to places that better catered to their habit.

The advantages of allowing the market, not government, to set up smoking rules—whether for the consumer or in the workplace—are numerous. First of all, with each entrepreneur making up his own rules, there may be in existence dozens, if not hundreds, of different methods of dealing with the problem of secondary smoke pollution. Given that the best means for solving the difficulty are yet to be discovered, leaving it up to the marketplace will likely maximize the chances for quickly uncovering the most efficient solution.

Secondly, the market process is more flexible than government intervention. There can usually be only one set of legislation in a given geographical area, but under free enterprise, businesses may be able to tailor their smoking rules to fit their widely diverging clientele. For example, it may well best suit the patrons of a pool hall, or bowling alley, or discotheque to allow smoking on the entire premises. The customers of this sort of establishment are least likely to object, and most likely to be comfortable in such circumstances. In contrast, health

food stores and vegetarian restaurants may only be able to survive by imposing a complete ban on all use of tobacco products. The market can accommodate both types of people, but it is difficult to see how coercive legislation can do so.

Thirdly, and perhaps most important, there is that often overlooked matter of freedom and individual liberty. Despite the desires of some people, the United States is still a country at least partially buttressed by the institution of private property. According to this doctrine, we are each of us the kings of our own little castles. It is thus our human right to be able to determine for ourselves how people must comport themselves in privately owned stores, restaurants, shopping centers, etc. If government is allowed to take over this realm and to dictate policy against the wishes of the owners of these establishments, then our liberty will be curtailed.

There is one argument, however, that directly challenges the freedom of every individual, but still has appeal in some quarters nevertheless. Under our present institutional arrangements of state subsidized health care, if a person contracts

cancer or emphysema or some other dread disease as a result of smoking, his care may be financially underwritten out of general tax funds. Under such circumstances, it is argued, the state has a right to insist that people maintain their health if only to avoid becoming a drain on the public purse.

The problem with this line of reasoning is that it puts the cart before the horse. The western democratic nations are supposedly predicated on the basic assumption that the state exists to serve the people's desires, not that the citizens exist in order to promote the interests of government. If people can be prohibited from smoking on the ground that the state finds inconvenient the resulting threat to their health, they can be forbidden to engage in any number of other potentially dangerous activities. But, do we really want a super nanny society which outlaws football, soccer, hockey, marathon running, triathlons, hang gliding, motorcycle riding, ice cream, candy, alcohol, and any and all other behavior which might put us at risk? Hardly. If push comes to shove, it would be far better to eliminate public funding of medical care, or at the very least allow people who insist on endangering their health in these ways to opt out.

12.

THE HUMAN-ORGAN MERCHANT

In the days of yore, there was no crisis in spare body parts. Organ transplants were an utter impossibility, the stuff of science fiction. Only Dr. Frankenstein and his literary ilk had any need for live organs.

But nowadays, thanks to the magnificent discoveries and new techniques of modern medicine, these possibilities are upon us. At present it is possible to transplant hearts, kidneys, livers, eyes, corneas, blood, bone marrow, and many other body parts. People who would have been consigned to death, or lingering, tenuous, and painful lives only a few short years ago can now avail themselves of these medical miracles and lead healthy, happy, productive lives.

All is not well, however, on the transplant front. Instead of being the occasion for unrelieved rejoicing, these new breakthroughs have brought in their train a whole host of problems.

First of all, there is a shortage of body organs suitable for transplant. Disease makes some of what is available unusable, along with incompatibility because of incompatible recipients' blood types.

This has led to a set of problems that has strained what passes for medical ethics in this country to the breaking point. For, given the limited supply of body parts, our doctors have had to pick and choose—on no criteria other than their own arbitrary whims—which of the many needy recipients shall have this life-giving aid, and which of them shall be denied. To this end, they place smokers, old people, and others less likely to benefit most from these operations at the end of the queue. In no other commercial setting, does anything like this occur. For example, the purveyors of groceries, automobiles, and books do not make such invidious distinctions between those more or less likely to gain advantage from their products.

The difficulty here is that our legal-economic system has not kept up with advancing medical technology. The law has prohibited people from using the property rights we each have in our own bodies. Specifically, it has banned trade, or a marketplace, in blood, bone marrow, and other live spare body parts.

I maintain that deregulation of this market is the solution to the transplant problem. But before I explain how free enterprise would work in this connection, let me lay a few fears to rest.

Yes, it is gory, disgusting, and very uncomfortable to discuss allowing profit incentives to work in this field. The very idea involves images of grave robbers, Frankenstein monsters, and gangs of "organ thieves" stealing people's hearts, livers, and kidneys in the manner described in several novels by Robin Cook. It seems cruel and unfeeling to discuss the market for used body parts in much the same manner we might use to describe the used-car market. But this is only because in our present society, while we can appreciate the miracles of modern medicine without necessarily comprehending them, we have such a poor understanding of the miracles of the marketplace that we cannot even begin to appreciate them. So let us sit back, relax, and calmly and dispassionately consider this idea on its own merits, all preconceptions and biases to one side. Let our only criteria be not our prejudice, unjustified

"... *INDUSTRIALS WERE UP AND UTILITIES HELD STEADY. LONDON GOLD CLOSED AT $453, UP $1.30 AND KIDNEYS CLOSED AT $12,725, UP $300 . . . .*"

in this case, but our assessment of whether this idea will really increase the number of donors, save lives and free doctors from the onerous decision of picking which needy people will be saved and which consigned to a lingering and painful death.

As any first year student in economics can tell you, whenever a good is in short supply, its price is too low. And the case of human organs is no exception. On the contrary, it is a paradigm case of this phenomenon. For our laws on this question, by prohibiting a marketplace from developing, have effectively imposed a zero price on these items.

But at a zero price, it should come as no surprise that the demand should vastly outstrip the supply. This, after all, is one of the most basic laws in all of economics. If the price were allowed to rise to its market clearing level, there might not be too great a change in the number of used body parts demanded. This is called by economists, "inelastic demand." All it means is that if you need a blood, bone marrow or organ transplant at all, price, no matter how high (within limits, of course), is not likely to deter you. No. The main effect of a free market in used body parts and fluids will be on the amount *supplied*.

How would such a marketplace actually work?

It is never possible to fully anticipate the functioning of an industry now prohibited by government edict. However, a few general principles become clear upon consideration.

We know that the major source of preferred organ donations will be young, healthy people who are cut down in the prime of life—by traffic accident, murder, war, heart attack, or in myriad other ways that leave their organs intact and reusable.

Were the industry to be legalized, new firms would spring up. Or perhaps, insurance companies or hospitals would expand their existing bases of operation. These firms would offer thousands of dollars to people who met the appropriate medical criteria and who would agree that, upon their demise, certain of their bodily organs would be owned by the businesses in question. Then they would turn around and sell these organs, at a profit, to people in need of transplants. In addition, these new firms would operate, as at present, to try to obtain consent from the relatives of newly deceased persons for use of their organs. Only now, under economic freedom, these firms would be in a position to offer cash incentives— as well as the chance to save another human life. In the case of blood, the Red Cross does, of course, pay for its supply. But its prices are too low, as shown by the fact that only insufficient quantities are brought forth. As well, it has failed to adopt a policy of differential prices to reflect the relative shortages of the various types of items needed. And there is no reason to believe that these private companies would not be able to increase the supply of this factor in accord with demand. Entrepreneurs in every other field of endeavor— some mundane, some exotic—have been able to accomplish this task with no fuss or fanfare.

Similarly, entrepreneurs in the human-organ business would be able to vastly increase the supply of donor organs. Certainly, many people all over the world would be happy to take advantage of the opportunity to cash in, while still alive, on the use of their vital organs after they had passed away. No one who objected—on religious grounds, for example— would have to cooperate with the venture. As a result, no longer would potential recipients have to make do without transplants. We need not even fear that those who engaged in this practice would earn "exorbitant" profits. For any such tendency would call forth new entrants into the field who would act so as to increase supply even further and reduce profits to levels which could be earned elsewhere.

There are hundreds, even thousands of people whose lives could be vastly improved today if they could but have the use of a healthy kidney. There are thousands of other people who die each year, taking perfectly healthy kidneys to the grave with them, who have no financial incentive at all to bequeath those organs to people in need. Why couldn't potential donors be given a pecuniary reward for doing the right thing?

Instead, our society must resort to all sorts of inefficient stratagems in an effort to get the transplantable organs to those who need them. Famous personages exhort us, in the event that we suffer untimely death, to make a posthumous gift of our kidneys. Medical schools coach their students on the best techniques for approaching next-of-kin; the difficulty is that they must ask permission at the precise time when they are least likely to be given it—upon the sudden demise of a loved one.

As a result, all of this has been to little avail. While potential recipients languish on painful kidney-dialysis machines, waiting ghoulishly for a traffic fatality that might spell life for them, the public refuses to sign cards in sufficient numbers giving permission for automatic posthumous donation of their kidneys. Things have even come to such a pass that there are grotesque and fascistic plans now being bruited about which would allow the government to seize the kidneys of accident victims unless they have signed cards denying permission for such seizure. The idea here is that if someone hasn't specifically demanded that he keep his property, then we can take it from him. But this justifies mugging, rape, theft, if the victim is too afraid to protest. When the state employs this vicious doctrine, there is also the implicit threat that government will turn against anyone who signs off from this list of "willing" donors. Critics of statist tyranny have often claimed that they are treated as if they are slaves of this institution. Seldom has any policy come closer to embodying this fear. This policy is predicated on the assumption that all organs (people?) really belong to the state.

The free enterprise system, were it allowed to operate in this instance, would be a Godsend to the unfortunate who suffer from diseased kidneys. A legal marketplace could encourage thousands of donors. Given free enterprise incentives, we would be—pardon the pun—up to our armpits in kidneys.

This is the tried and true process we rely upon to bring us all the other necessities of life: food, clothing, and shelter. We do not depend upon voluntary donations for the provision of these goods and services.

Neither do we depend upon black markets to provide us with food, clothing, and shelter. But under present circumstances, when voluntary donations prove inadequate, we *do* have to depend upon illegal sales for transplantable organs. According to some estimates, the black market value of a transplantable kidney is between $50,000 and $100,000—worth much more than its weight in gold.

The question is, is such an underground body-parts supplier a benefit or a detriment? One argument for the latter view is that the black marketeer, if successful, will tend to undermine respect for law and order. He is, after all, thumbing his nose at the duly constituted authorities, who have so far remained adamant in declaring such "ghoulish" sales and purchases

"I'LL HAVE THE IMPORTED SWISS, TYPE O POSITIVE, TRIPLE SUPER-SCREENED FOR AIDS AND HEPATITIS B, PREFERABLY FROM THE CANTON OF SCHAFFHAUSEN."

illegal. As against that, it could be argued that any legal code which, in effect if not by intention, consigns innocent individuals to death or to lives of misery on kidney-dialysis machines richly deserves to be ignored.

But one point is clear. Our black market "ghoul" benefits organ donors by offering them financial remuneration as well as the satisfaction of knowing that the organs they may donate upon their demise will enable others to live. By doing this, he will also, as we have seen, increase the number of organs available, and this will be of inestimable benefit to those who might otherwise have been forced to go without.

Let's allow free enterprise to work in the field of blood, bone marrow, and transplantable organs and save us all a lot of pain, sorrow, suffering, and tragedy.

One objection to the foregoing is that if we allowed market prices for these commodities, organ thieves would arise. They would steal into our bedrooms in the dead of night and seize our livers, lungs, hearts, etc. This objection is based upon economic illiteracy, however. The payoff to and therefore the temptation for such body snatching will depend upon the *price* of the goods in question. But, the present black market price of these body parts is much *higher* than would be the free market price. Why so? Because while demand would stay the same, the *supply* of the organs would be greater in a regime of economic freedom. Thus, if there is any danger of these ghoulish goings on, it is right *now*, with a price control of zero. That is to say, the risk of body snatching would be *lower* in a regime of economic freedom than at present.

Let me conclude this chapter with the only argument I have ever been able to uncover in *favor* of the present vicious system. (They don't call me Walter "Fair and Balanced" Block for nothing, you know.) It is this: the extant prohibition of a free market in human organs creates great drama for movies and television. Will the cute little boy get his heart transplant before he dies or not? Will the potential recipient be able to stop smoking, so that the nanny state doctors will give him a new liver? Without price controls of zero, these occurrences will be part and parcel of our medieval system. Playwrights will have one less source of drama.

13.

BREAST MILK
SUBSTITUTE PURVEYOR

The so-called infant formula crisis is yet another stick used by critics of the market to beat up on the free enterprise system. Exhibit "A" in their indictment is the fact that manufacturers of this product sell it in powder form in poverty-stricken Third World countries. The problem there, is that the water the baby formula is mixed with is impure. Thus, the result of mixing the powder and this water is harmful to the infants.

But why blame the marketplace? There has not ever been so much as a hint that there is any problem with the breast milk substitute itself. No, it has always been beyond reproach. The sole cause of the problem is, instead, the *water*. And, who, pray tell, is in charge of water supply? The free enterprise system? Not a bit of it. Rather, it is the state apparatus that has arrogated to itself control of this "vital body fluid". Thus, the responsibility for the failure of breast milk substitutes lies in the so-called public sector, not in the private one.

Nor are our friends, the leftist critics of capitalism, at all apologetic about this. No. Any call for the privatization of the water supply is likely to be met with derision and worse by them. Should we turn reservoirs over to the tender mercies of profits, greed, and markets? Not in their view. Instead, they have a perverse hatred for that small bit of this market that has been taken over by entrepreneurs: bottled water. The temerity of these people. They blame a private product for misery, when it is government provision that is at fault. Often, they do their utmost to ban the innocent, privately manufactured powder, while doing their utmost to protect the real culprit of the piece, government control over water supplies.

Exhibit "B" in the case against the use of infant formula is the fact that hospitals often give these products away for free to the mothers of newborns. This encourages the parents to use it, one, because it is free, and two, because it comes with the imprimatur of the medical profession.

Now, let us sit back and contemplate all this for a moment.

First, market opponents are forever criticizing laissez faire for encouraging greed, profits, high prices, etc. Along comes an institution that provides something, not only at a low price but for *free*, and what is their reaction? Thankfulness? No. The very opposite. Secondly, while natural breast milk is indeed in most cases considerably superior to the chemical substitute, there are some women who are unable to breast feed. For them, instant milk is a Godsend. Even for mothers who can function in this regard, the baby formula can still serve as a supplement to the natural process. Are these women to be penalized because some ignorant and/or uncaring mothers will undoubtedly abuse this product? If so, then we might as well ban alcohol, chocolate, ice cream, hot dogs, French fries, because some irresponsible people will indulge in them to excess and hurt themselves and/or their babies.

Giving things away like this is only the tip of the iceberg. Loss leaders, or outright freebies on a temporary basis, are indeed a ploy of companies to enter new markets. How better to encourage people unfamiliar with a product than to charge a spectacularly low price for it or give it away. Since *any* item can be used to excess, and thus prove harmful (dosage is all), the logic of opposition to making a gift of infant formula is to ban low prices or giveaways for *anything*. One wonders if these market critics would accept this logical implication of their stance.

What about the problem regarding the Chinese baby formula that supposedly had poison in it. As a result, many young children were killed, it is claimed. Does this not give us pause for thought before defunding purveyors of this product?

No.

This can happen with anything consumed by human beings. Artificial breast milk? Yes. But also, apples, bread, lima beans, steaks, ice cream, you name it. Should the government be placed in charge of all foodstuffs, medicines, etc., on the grounds that the market is imperfect, and that some people will be killed by it?

There are problems with such a solution. First, the problem with the Chinese baby formula occurred in 2008. Laissez faire capitalism was hardly in operation at that place or time. China, despite its magnificent strides in that direction, is not yet the paradigm case of free enterprise. As for the importation of this dangerous product to the U.S., the governmental Food and Drug Administration (FDA) bore full responsibility for allowing this disaster to occur.

The market has many advantages vis-à-vis government certification of safety, whether for food, drugs or any other product. When failures occur (and they can take place under *either* institutional arrangement, public or private), there is an automatic feedback mechanism at work in the market: loss of money and eventual bankruptcy. This does not work in the government sector. No matter how many lives the FDA has ruined, it is still in business.

Yes, some people will undoubtedly perish by using products that emanate from the private sector. That is the penalty for not living in the Garden of Eden. But more, many more, will do so if these tasks are given over to the statist bureaucrats.

Having established our thesis on this matter, let us now deal with an objection to it, from a very influential group.

According to the Infant Formula Action Coalition (INFACT), several multinational corporations were guilty of launching an aggressive advertising campaign, aimed at selling breast milk substitutes to Third World mothers. This had led to an outbreak of infant deaths from "baby bottle disease," because, while the product may be perfectly acceptable in Europe or North America, this does not hold for the Third World. The reasons: 1) the water supplies there are usually polluted, so the infant formula is mixed with impure water, with deleterious effects; 2) severe poverty makes it difficult to buy the fuel necessary to boil and sterilize the water; 3) Third World mothers can't afford to buy sufficient amounts of formula to replace their own milk—they must therefore dilute the formula well beyond the point called for in the written instructions; 4) they do not refrigerate the milk, also contrary to instructions, since very few own refrigerators; and 5) by the time the mother realizes that infant formula leads to a sickly, malnourished baby, her own milk has dried up and she has no alternative but to continue formula usage.

It is presumably for these or similar reasons that many critics of multinational enterprise also approve of Third World or international (United Nations) efforts to better govern the practices of transnational pharmaceutical companies.

The implicit premise of the argument is that as bad as these practices of the multinationals are, the efforts of the various U.N. organizations would not be worse. But, when looked at in this way, such a claim is very difficult to sustain.

For it is conceded by INFACT and other opponents of the multinationals that there is nothing wrong with baby formula *per se*. The difficulty concerns only the economic situation in the Third World with which the formula must interact: the poverty, the impure water, the illiteracy, the lack of refrigeration, etc.

But which organizations are responsible for this sad state of affairs in the first place? The collectivist economic planning of the Third World socialist governments (and the U.N.) is itself accountable for the poverty, the impure water, the illiteracy, the lack of refrigeration, etc., which are the root causes of the infant formula tragedy. Asking the Third World governments, or the U.N., to take charge and improve matters, is thus akin to asking the arsonist to put out the fire.

Let us now consider a second argument against government control of pharmaceutical multinationals, again on the assumption that the scenario given by INFACT is accurate.

We live in a sea of ignorance. On this side of the Garden of Eden, even with the best of intentions, men are likely to err. Their mistakes are liable to be serious, even, upon occasion, causing the deaths of numerous people. There is nothing that can be done to alter this unfortunate situation; it follows directly from man's imperfection.

There is, however, one (admittedly imperfect) remedy: if we cannot eliminate this error, let us *at least* resolve to adopt a system which automatically and quickly rewards people who are *less* liable to make such mistakes and discourages those who are more prone to make them. The marketplace is far preferable in this regard than the regulatory bureaus which are very indirectly controlled through the political process. In order to further cement this insight, we consider yet another multinational pharmaceutical tragedy which rivals even the milk substitute horror: the thalidomide case.

Now thalidomide (a morning sickness drug that causes birth defects) was produced by a private company and approved for use by the West German regulatory bureau concerned with pharmaceuticals. Given this horrendous mistake, how have the two fared? Which one was forced to cease and desist: the private company, by the marketplace, or the West

German regulatory bureau, through the political process? Obviously, it was the former. The latter, although co-responsible for the tragedy, is still operating. A similar point can be made for the Vichyssoise soup company, which quickly went out of business after causing several deaths by poisoning, while the FDA, which oversees all such companies is still doing business at the same old lemonade stand quite nicely, thank you.

Having assumed, arguendo, the accuracy of the INFACT story, it is now time to challenge it. According to the infant formula protesters, the manufacturer's advertising is responsible for the adoption of breast milk alternatives in the Third World. Yet there is little statistical correlation between advertising efforts and infant formula use.

Then there was the widely touted claim that "up to one million infant deaths per year are attributable to infant formula." However, as it turned out, the "evidence" for this claim was a "symbolic figure"; i.e., one made up out of whole cloth by an anti-infant formula activist. The problem with this "up to" claim is that it is true even if zero, one, two or three deaths occurred as a result. If John ate one pickle, it is *true* that John ate "up to 1,000,000 pickles." This is demagoguery.

IV. SEX

14.

TOPLESS IN PUBLIC

T he feminists have had their comeuppance, and they don't much like it.

Several women in both the U.S. and Canada have won court rulings that they could bare their breasts at public parks and swimming pools. They have brought suit under "classical" feminist theory that men and women are in all respects alike, entitled to the same rights, and that since men are permitted by law to go topless in such venues, so must this apply to women.

Some self-styled feminists are spluttering mad. This is no way to achieve equality, they groan. Rather, it will be a field day for exhibitionists on the one hand, and men who like to leer. It will be no fun for the rest of us either, the ones trying to raise young children, or who wish for a modicum of decorum on moral, cultural or aesthetic grounds. For make no mistake about it: this is only the entering wedge. There is little doubt that other women will bring similar suits, and judges will go along with them, if these precedents hold. Today, parks and swimming pools; tomorrow, these places plus anywhere else that men customarily take off their tee shirts; on the basketball

court (shirts vs. skins), on the sidewalk on a hot day, at the beach, playing baseball, etc.

Nor can one really fault these exhibitionist feminists. True, the female chest is fraught with sexuality in a way that does not apply to men (contrary to feminists, there are some very strong biological differences between the genders), but rights are rights. Why shouldn't females have the right to go topless that men so cavalierly assume?

Non-feminists are not all pleased with this new spate of judicial findings either. The female breast, it would appear, is not conducive to morality, to family formation and other desiderata of the conservative right. An exception is sometimes made in this quarter for breastfeeding, but otherwise toplessness is seen as immoral flaunting. Another arrow in this particular quiver is the claim that such lewd behavior will lead to rape: men, it seems, are unable to control their savage impulses at the sight of a naked breast. However, if this were true, we would have to ban not only being half dressed, but also short or tight skirts, low-cut blouses, etc. This way lies making the burqa compulsory for all women; and that is hardly a policy in keeping with libertarian notions of freedom.

The cause of the social problem, and a hint as to its solution, are private property rights. These new judicial dispensations apply only to *public* property. There is no possibility, at least if private property rights are respected, that women will be able to bare their bosoms, even though men are allowed to, on private golf courses, or amusement parks or shopping malls or stores if the owner of these facilities oppose such semi un-dress. If McDonalds can refuse service to anyone not wearing shoes, they can do so, at least in the free society, for anyone not attired as desired by this corporation.

And herein lies the hint as to how we can have our cake and eat it, too. How we, as a society, need not treat women any differently than men, and yet can attain a minimal level of sartorial decency: privatize all property; roads, beaches, parks, athletic fields, streets, sidewalks, swimming pools, whatever! Then, private enterprise will handle the rest. Conceivably, there might be some few emporia that allow women to go shirtless when men do, but, likely, these would be very few and far apart. For in the marketplace, the customer is king. If the overwhelming majority wish to maintain a difference between male and female attire, then virtually all entrepreneurs will have to cater to their taste or face a swift and certain bankruptcy (well, assuming no government bailouts). But the tiny minority that wishes to disport itself on the basis of splendid equality between the sexes can also have its way; for surely there will arise on the market business firms willing to cater to their tastes, too.

In this way, in one fell swoop, we obviate the entire debate as to whether women have the right to expose the top half of their bodies. In that direction lie endless arguments over the number of angels dancing on the tips of pins. With no possible rights violation, we confine such behavior to the small percentage of property likely to be utilized by people of this taste. Otherwise, we allow a very small minority to discomfort the rest of society.

There are other side benefits as well. With all property in private hands, the level of safety will rise, as Disneyland type police are much more beholden to their employers, and through them, to the consumer, than are the cops who refused to stop the "wildings" in New York City's Central Park. Traffic fatalities, too, can be expected to plummet, as we change over from a roadway transportation system which can only be described as "Sovietized" to one more compatible with our basic institutions of private property. (On this see my book Block, Walter. 2009. *The Privatization of Roads and Highways: Human and Economic Factors;* Auburn, AL: The Mises Institute; http://mises.org/books/roads_web.pdf.)

15.

POLYGAMOUS MARRIAGE

What is the libertarian perspective on polygamous marriage? Whether it's polygyny (a man with more than one wife) or polyandry (a woman with more than one husband), or group marriage (where several wives and husbands marry one another), the libertarian response is the same as it is on anything and everything else. If the institution constitutes a *per se* violation of the non-aggression principle, it should be prohibited; if it does not, then it should be legal.

So, does a man marrying numerous wives necessarily involve aggression against them? It is difficult to see how and why this should be so. Of course, in some societies women are forced into marriage against their will. This is certainly contrary to libertarian law, and should be ended forthwith. But marriage coercion can occur no matter how many wives are involved. It cannot be denied that in some societies, under-aged girls are abducted and married off without their proper consent. But again, this takes place under both polygamy and monogamy. The problem at least for the libertarian concerns the coercion, not the number of wives.

Is polygamy socially dangerous, in that the children from marriages with multiple spouses engage in more truancy, delinquency, drug use, etc., than the progeny emanating from other institutional arrangements? There is no evidence for any such claim. Even if there were, even if there were a clear pattern in this regard, this would still not justify a legitimate reason to ban the practice. Black children suffer from this sort of malady to a greater degree than others. According to the pernicious "logic" that would outlaw polygamous marriages, this should be applied, too, to marriages within the African American community, a truly preposterous result.

No, marriage, in the libertarian society, would be handled like any other business partnership. Anyone may marry one or as many (adult) spouses as he wishes, provided, only, that there is mutual consent.

Men die sooner than women; not only is their life expectancy shorter, but they succumb to a greater degree than women at all times, due to crime (either as perpetrators or victims), accidents or illness. Thus, at any decade of life there are typically fewer husbands available than wives. This is a particular plight for black women. A disproportionate number of the black men they would otherwise be likely to marry are incarcerated or dead. Thus, polygamy has some advantages over monogamy, at least insofar as maximizing the number of people who can be married and reducing the number of people who will necessarily be consigned to live unconnected with this institution. The Chinese policy of one child per couple has eventuated in a relative "oversupply" of males compared to females. The implication of this brutal policy would incline us toward multiple marriages.

Needless to say, but we will say it anyway, this mutual consent criterion would apply to gay marriage. It seems logically inconsistent to allow same-sex marriages, but to prohibit them between groups of heterosexuals. People are people, of whatever variety of sexual preferences *or* numbers involved. It is a source of amusement to find that those who favor legalizing homosexual marriages oppose polygamy, and vice versa. That is, commentators who support heterosexual polygamy often reject marriage for gays. Why can't we all just get along, and allow all consenting adults to do whatever it is they wish to do, either alone, or with one other person, or with many people, provided, of course, that no rights are thereby violated?

If we really oppose polygamy, we ought to reconsider our position on serial monogamy, which is now entirely within the law. At present, a man may marry as many women (who will have him) as he wishes, and, of course, vice versa. There is no real upper bound, except for life expectancy. For example, he could start at age twenty, and continue, say, until he was seventy, marrying one woman per year, divorcing her within twelve months and then starting in again with the next Mrs. on his dance card. If so, he would have had fifty wives. (He might be a bit confused, but that is another matter.) There must be very few polygamists who are married to over four dozen women at any given time. Yet, what is the real difference between polygamy at any one time, and polygamy over time, that is, serial monogamy? Does anyone favor placing an upper limit on the number of monogamous marriages a person may enter into? Elizabeth Taylor, Larry King, call your congressman.

16.

BURNING BED

In 1984, NBC presented a made-for-TV movie, "The Burning Bed." Starring the late Farrah Fawcett, it told the story of Francine Hughes, a woman who had been beaten by her husband for 13 years. Finally, the battered wife soaked her sleeping husband's bed with gasoline, lit a match and burned him to death.

Right after the broadcast of this movie, violence occurred in three separate cities in the U.S. In Milwaukee, thirty-nine-year-old Joseph Brandt waited for his estranged thirty-seven-year-old wife, Sharon, in her driveway. When she pulled up, he doused her with gasoline and threw a lighted match at her. In Quincy, Massachusetts, a husband became enraged by the show and beat his wife to a bloody pulp. According to the director of the shelter that took her in, the husband told her he wanted to get her before she got him. And in Chicago, as if to feed the fears of this Quincy husband, a battered wife watched "The Burning Bed" and shot her husband with a pistol.

Nor was this the only case of life imitating art. In Portsmouth, Virginia, a man watched the movie "Revenge of the Ninja," a story about a Japanese assassin. Depressed over his families' eviction from their home, twenty-four-year-old Gregory

"MR. SIEGAL, IT'S SOME WOMAN WHO WATCHED OUR RE-RUN OF 'THE BURNING BED' LAST NIGHT. SHE WANTS TO KNOW ABOUT HOW MUCH GASOLINE DID THE WIFE USE."

Eley donned oriental garb and battle stars, armed himself with a submachine gun, two crossbows and a hand gun, and murdered a woman who had sued him over a business deal.

A question not unnaturally arises. Should society ban movies which feature themes of death and destruction, which may lead people to emulate them? It is easy to advocate censorship, for, had these two movies not been shown, several people may not have been killed.

But a moment's reflection casts doubt on such a public policy decision. If we banned movies, we would have to ban books, stories, paintings, plays, operas, etc. Even children's fairy tales – *Jack and the Bean Stalk, Little Red Riding Hood, Chicken Little, Hansel and Gretel* – are replete with mayhem and murder. Down this path lies the end of culture and art as we know it.

But there is an even more basic objection to censorship and prior restraint. The human being is a creature of free will. People, whether they like it or not, are responsible for their own acts. "The Burning Bed" and all other artistic endeavours that depict violence are not to blame for the acts of those who chose to emulate them. Only the criminals themselves are responsible and guilty.

As to prior restraint, we know that the wild celebrations that follow any significant world sporting event sometimes result in deaths, either out of exhuberance, or, sometimes, unruly hooligans. If we follow the "logic" here, we would have to ban all such athletic events, surely something that should give us pause. It would be insufficient to prohibit, merely, celebratory parades afterward; the enthusiasm of these sports fans would likely overcome any such attempt. Moreover, the hoodlums who engage in mayhem at these times are pretty well known in terms of demography: males from their teens until the end of their twenties. We could save lives with a little "prior restraint" here: throw all males into jail at age 15 or so, and throw away the key until they have reached three decades of age.

Sounds silly, does it not? But, the same reasoning applies to censoring movies, plays, and literature even if it could be shown that they incite violence.

More recently, in Tucson, a crazed gunman murdered six people and wounded thirteen others, including U.S. Rep. Gabrielle Giffords. In a blood libel launched by "progressives," this tragedy was widely blamed upon Glen Beck, Rush Limbaugh, Sarah Palin, and other conservatives for their "vitriolic" political speech. Should we prohibit commentators who occupy the right wing part of the spectrum from speaking out? This is just as problematic. Surely, the call for precisely that result might well be regarded as "hateful," and thus, if the logic of the leftist critics is employed, they would be hoist by their own petard: their very charges would be deemed illegal based on the laws they themselves favor.

V. DISCRIMINATORS

17.

THE SEXIST

In the good old days, the idea of human rights was clear. We all had the right not to be murdered, not to be tortured, not to be raped, not to be kidnapped, not to be robbed, not to be trespassed upon, and not to be victimized by other crimes such as assault and battery, fraud, pickpocketing, and other such felonies. These were all negative rights; others had the obligation to *refrain* from violating our persons or properties.

But nowadays, we are under the influence of the new so-called human rights philosophy. These activists have introduced an entirely new set of positive rights. According to this view, we now have a right to medical care, to decent housing, to adequate schooling and to a certain level of income. There are even "welfare rights" organizations organized to demand welfare payments from the rest of society, not as a form of charity, but as a "right."

All of this new human rights blather really has nothing at all to do with rights. Instead, it is a fraudulent attempt to trade in on a widely respected concept—rights—and to try to smuggle in under this guise an entirely different and hidden agenda, that of egalitarianism or wealth redistribution. Let us

"YOUR AD READS, 'SHORT, WHITE, MALE PROTESTANT ON THE
HEAVY SIDE WANTS TO MEET WHITE PROTESTANT WOMAN,
30-40, FOR SERIOUS RELATIONSHIP.' I'M SORRY, SIR, THE
HUMAN RIGHTS CODE WILL ONLY PERMIT, 'PERSON WANTS TO
MEET PERSON FOR SEX.' "

consider how very different the two concepts are: the old view
of negative rights and the new one concerning positive rights.

Under the old concept, people were asked only to refrain
from certain antisocial and pernicious actions. They could
not murder, rape or steal. Under the new concept, individuals are not asked to refrain from anything. Rather, they are
forced to give of themselves, their time and their money, in
order to make their own wealth available for the purposes of
other people.

Another difference. If all of mankind were so inclined, it
could, at one fell swoop, end all violations of negative rights.
That is, through a sheer act of will, we could all resolve to end
murder, rape, and theft, instantaneously. All it would take is
a *decision* on the part of all of us. In contrast, no such thing is

possible in the realm of positive rights. Even with the best will in the world, there is no possibility of ending the miserable, grinding poverty—most of which is brought about, I might add, by an excess of this egalitarian philosophy—in many of the countries of the Third World.

A third difference. If I have more of my positive rights met, you have less of yours met. If more money is spent for food for you, less remains to be spent for me. For positive rights are really a demand for wealth redistribution. In contrast, if less theft is perpetrated on me, it is not at all necessary that more be perpetrated on you. As we have seen, robbery can be reduced merely by an act of will. Similarly, if I have more free speech or more freedom to worship, you need not have less of these things.

A fourth. There is no reductio ad absurdum for negative rights. All their advocate has to do is refrain from invasions, uninvited border crossings. In contrast, the proponent of positive rights—who has more wealth than the average person on earth—has to explain why he has not voluntarily followed his own proscription and donated this "excess" amount to the poor. Presumably, the blind man who has no eyes would benefit from the receipt of this body part more than would the donor lose from such a transaction. And, yet, there are proponents of positive rights who have not made this transfer. So, the next time you see an egalitarian, look him straight in the eye. If he has two of them, he is a hypocrite.

When you hear anyone complaining about our vanishing human rights, ask yourself if they are talking about real (negative) rights violations or are they just unhappy that there are now fewer coerced transfers of wealth?

Whenever there is a discussion about reducing the power of a so called human rights commission, the trendy lefties typically unleash such sound and fury that you might be excused for thinking that Genghis Khan was now in charge of rights and liberties.

"THE WORD 'MALE' MUST BE
REMOVED - THE REST CAN STAY."

An example of this is the "human rights" industry's refusal to allow an old lady to advertise for a "good Christian boarder," on the grounds, presumably, that this discriminated against bad, non-Christian boarders. But doesn't she have the right to choose anyone she wants as a boarder? What will be next: telling women who they have to befriend? Who they must marry? Another example, this one from Canada, is their hounding of one small Vancouver business, Hunky Bill's Perogies, whose proprietor's only "crime" was to insist on his right to name his own enterprise in any manner he chose. (It would appear that the name "Hunky" is offensive to some; well, if so, let them not patronize the establishment.) Moreover, these so called "human rights" boards refused to allow a private golf club to reserve the course for men only on one day per week. One commission even refused to allow a shop selling clothing for tall women to advertise for a tall female salesclerk. Presumably, this discriminates against salesclerks who are short and male. It is interesting to note, however, that no similar objection is typically made to feminist conferences — which prohibit attendance by men.

Feminists are hypocritical. They are sometimes intent, not in acting on behalf of a discrimination-free society, as one might expect, but in favor of a society segregated on the basis of gender. To wit, a female-only conference on the media, organized by groups ostensibly opposed to sexual segregation. But according to a conference organizer, men were excluded because a number of male journalists had already been interviewed on the subject of the media. Evidently, the male reporter who had tried to cover a weekend session, but was told to leave, was not one of those who had "already been interviewed." According to a spokesman [sic!] for this event, this occurrence "was an attempt to include women rather than exclude men." Put that in your pipe and smoke it, male chauvinist pigs of the world!

Nor did this bit of illogic exhaust the explanatory powers of the women's movement. According to a managing editor of *Herizons* [sic], a women's news magazine, the decision to exclude men was a form of affirmative action: "It's really important that women catch up in this field, and of course the logical place to give them opportunity is at a women's conference."

Can anyone imagine what the response of the professional feminists, and all others in the "human rights" biz, would have been had a group of male Anglo-Saxon protestants used a similar line of argument to justify the exclusion of females, or homosexuals, or native peoples, or handicapped persons, or, indeed, any other group favored by current fashions?

"...YOU HAVE A RIGHT TO REMAIN SILENT, A RIGHT TO LEGAL COUNSEL, A RIGHT TO MAKE A PHONE CALL, A RIGHT TO DECENT, AFFORDABLE HOUSING, FREE MEDICAL CARE, EDUCATION, DAY CARE, AND DEPENDING ON YOUR GENDER, A FREE ABORTION, A RIGHT TO ...."

The very use of the phrase "human rights" by these people is an outrageous presumption. These exercises in frivolity have as much to do with human rights as fish do with bicycles—to mention an aphorism beloved of the so called feminists. For people do have a human right to discriminate. Must the homosexual nightclub be forced to hire women? Must the lesbian restaurant or social club be forced to hire men? Must Chinese restaurants be forced to hire non-oriental cooks and waiters?

And what of Catholics, Orthodox Jews, and members of the Russian Orthodox Church? Their religious principles forbid the ordination of women. But this is incompatible with the human rights legislation which compels hiring irrespective of sex. It is the sheerest effrontery to link legislation denying these religious freedoms with "human rights."

Heterosexuals are truly disgusting in that they discriminate against half the human race in terms of love-interest candidates. Male heterosexuals eliminate all men in this regard; female heterosexuals disregard all other members of the fairer sex. The same is true for the equally repulsive and discriminating homosexuals. They, too, are equally repulsive. Lesbians will not contemplate a romantic relationship with a man. Male homosexuals will not consider such with a woman. It is only the bisexual who passes muster as far as sexism is concerned. They are open to relationships with anyone. Thus, the case against sexism is really a not-so-hidden call for compulsory bisexuality, at least insofar as its advocates wish to write it into law. Of course, they, too, are despicable persons; bisexuals discriminate on the basis of "lookism," sense of humor, intelligence, accomplishments and other such attributes. Where, oh where, are we to find even one fully honest man on the basis of this perverted criterion?

18.

PEEPING TOM

We live in an era where privacy is exalted, at least insofar as the law is concerned. So called privacy rights are entrenched in law and supported by pundits. What is the right to privacy? It is the right that no one else shall know about your business; that you can remain anonymous if you wish to do so, that you are able to fly under the radar, that no one can see you unless you wish to be seen, among other things.

Even at first glance, there is something very problematic about this concept. For at one fell swoop it would prohibit detectives who are perhaps the greatest violators of privacy of them all. Were privacy to be supreme, and this were exported to the world of fiction, then none of the following could have come into being: Lew Archer, Elijah Baley, Batman, Harry Bosch, Dr. Temperance "Bones" Brennan, Father Brown, Brother Cadfael, Joe Caneili, Chen Cao, Rex Carver, Charlie Chan, Ellah Clah, Inspector Clouseau, Columbo, Elvis Cole, Alex Cross, R. Daneel Olivaw, Rick Deckard, Harry Dresden, Nancy Drew, Jessica Fletcher, Dan Fortune, Mike Hammer, Hardy Boys, Cliff Hardy, Sherlock Holmes, Miss Marple, Thomas Magnum, Philip Marlowe, Veronica Mars, Perry Mason, Travis

McGee, Kinsey Millhone, Adrian Monk, Stephanie Plum, Hercule Poirot, Laura Principal, Precious Ramotswe, Sunny Randall, Ezekiel "Easy" Rawlins, Jack Reacher, Jim Rockford, Father (later Bishop) "Blackie" Ryan, John Shaft, Rabbi David Small, Sam Spade, Spenser, Jesse Stone, Brother William of Baskerville, V. I. Warshawski, and Nero Wolfe. My apologies to the authors and fans of those who were left off this list; send me the missing names, and I'll stick them into the next edition of this book. It is hard to believe that in a world where privacy was actually a right, all of these famous detectives would have been confined to oblivion. Or, that their actions, qua detectives, were entirely illegal. Yet, it is difficult to draw any other conclusion. Nor are detectives the only ones who would be banned by law under the "privacy rights" doctrine. There are others who turn over rocks and look for worms: journalists, historians, gossips and all those who attempt to get behind facades and permeate the veil of ignorance. Inquiring minds want to know, and these are the people who help us satisfy our quest for such knowledge. A large part of what a detective, historian, or journalist (e.g., Julian Assange) does is attempting to unearth secrets, publicizing what his targets have done, which the latter would just as soon keep hidden from widespread perusal. It cannot be right that all of these efforts should be illegal. Certainly, we cannot want to prohibit by law all attempts to find out what a person does that he wishes to be kept to himself.

According to the libertarian legal code, we may do *anything* at all to each other, whether they like it or not, provided, only, that in so doing we not violate—not their privacy "rights" which do not exist, but rather—their *property* rights in their own persons and justly owned physical possessions. If the historian or gossip does that, he is acting contrary to the privacy proviso. But he may do anything else he wishes to do, as long as he operates within this boundary.

So, may a detective, hired by a wife, target a husband to determine whether or not he is committing adultery? Yes, as long as the gumshoe does not commit a trespass, or any other such rights violation. May the detective use binoculars or even a telescope if he wishes to engage in long distance surveillance? Yes, of course. If the journalist may look at his target with the naked eye, he most certainly may also utilize technical aids. No one seriously objects to the use of eyeglasses or opera glasses. The purpose to which they are being put should be irrelevant (again, assuming no rights violations). In Robert B. Parker's book *Night and Day* (2009), fictional Paradise, Massachusetts, Police Chief Jesse Stone contends with Mrs. Betsy Ingersoll, the principal of a local school. She forced eighth-grade girls to go to their locker room, raise their dresses and reveal their underwear. Did this "educator" violate the girls' privacy? This would appear to be a paradigm case of just that offense. How would such an invasion be dealt with in the libertarian society? Any private school would lose customers if it treated its young customers in such a manner. Obviously, it would forbid such invasions of privacy on the part of its administrators, and, if they disobeyed, would summarily fire them. What about "magic" eyeglasses that enable the wearer to see through clothes, and even bricks and cement, providing a sort of X-ray vision of the sort Superman boasted? Yes to this, too, since the object of the search has no right to privacy or anything else that would count against it.

Some airports now use similar but less powerful technology. Is this justified? No. For this is based upon a quid pro quo requirement (if you are not willing to succumb to this electronic invasion, you are denied permission to fly), and those who impose it (the government) have no right, under the libertarian law code, to do any such thing. On the other hand, if a purely private airport, or airline, made such a demand, it most certainly would have the *right* to subject would-be passengers to such an intimate search. It is their private property, after all. Those who do not want to be subjected to such a loss of privacy are free to go elsewhere. And, given a market system, and most people's antipathy to having their privacy disrespected in such a manner, it is safe to say that this would confer a competitive advantage on entrepreneurs who forego the use of such machinery. On the other hand, if this technology promotes safety, and the consumer values that over any embarrassment suffered being seen *au naturel*, then the marketplace might well adopt it.

Suppose there are defensive responses available, for example, lead could block Superman's X-ray vision. Or perhaps a "magic" cloaking device will one day be invented. Would the target be within his rights to utilize such a preventative technology? Of course (and he may indeed do so, provided only the property owner does not demand he forego this right as a requirement for entry). But let us get back to the real world for a moment. If A looks at B, the latter has no right to prevent this. "He is looking at me" is not a sufficient claim to justify the intervention of the forces of law and order to stop it. So, yes, people are not required to live in all-glass houses (with no curtains), or dress in a manner that enables all and sundry to view their entire bodies.

How, then, shall we regard the "peeping Tom." He uses his right to open his eyes and look around the world in a salacious manner. His perusal of naked and half-naked ladies, to be sure, does not pass the "smell test." It is certainly morally objectionable. But, were this activity to be outlawed, then so would all "eye to breast" contact, something of which virtually every heterosexual man would be guilty, and for a significant proportion of most waking hours. Now, of course, there are differences between the peeping Tom and normal males. But these consist, mainly, of the fact that the former will engage in trespass, and the latter will not. But, we already, quite properly, have laws on the books that prohibit entering onto other people's property, whether or not for the purpose of illicitly viewing them. So, peeping Tomism is not *per se*, properly, a crime. Rather, trespassing is. If the peeping Tom would eschew trespass, then, as far as libertarian law is concerned, he could engage in peeping to his heart's content. But does not such activity lead to more serious crimes, such as rape? Would not society be justified in banning it on that ground alone? Well, no. If so, Victoria's Secret would be against the law, as would any movie or book that led some deranged soul to commit a crime. It is indeed a "blood libel" to accuse Sarah Palin, Rush Limbaugh or Glenn Beck of the horrendous murders in Arizona *even if* their actions did indeed "lead" unhinged Jared Loughner to do them, for which no scintilla of evidence exists.

There is a further issue to be considered. An awful lot of peeping takes place on the streets and sidewalks of the nation. These Toms have every right to be on these premises; this is a great aid to their habits. What is to be done? In the libertarian society, there would be no such thing as a public street or sidewalk. All would be privatized. (See my book *The Privatization of Roads and Highways.*) Presumably, their private owners would prohibit such activity. End of problem, in one fell swoop, apart from peeping from helicopters, or from one building to another, etc.

If we lived in a different kind of world, where merely looking at others created physical harm to them, then and only then would doing so be properly characterized as an invasion. In such a world, we would be forced by law to avert our eyes from each other, unless we had permission (that is, only sadists would view masochists).

Let us now consider the issue of men looking under the skirts of women who are above them on staircases, and/or photographing them in such revealing positions. This is yet another paradigm case of a privacy violation. Stipulate that females wish to avoid being exhibited in such a manner. Given this, entrepreneurs will compete with one another so as to design staircases where such viewing is greatly attenuated, and/or impossible. A similar situation occurs with school desks placed in the hollow square format. Privacy barriers on such desks are placed so as to promote modesty in this regard. On the other hand, let us suppose that men prefer staircases and desks unencumbered. If they are willing to pay enough money for this privilege, it is possible that an entrepreneur might be able to subsidize females sufficiently to overcome their distaste for being exhibited in this way. But, certainly, in no libertarian society would owners of staircases and desks be held criminally or tortuously liable for failure to protect ladies from unwanted male glimpses of them. The rule would be, anyone can look anywhere he wants to, unless, the private property owner rules against this. When it comes to looking from one piece of property to another, even with the aid of binoculars, merely looking cannot be considered an invasion.

How would the problem of the paparazzi be handled in the free society? Or, should famous movie stars, professional athletes, top selling musicians and their ilk be forced to endure swarms of hooligans armed with cameras getting into their faces? (I am now assuming that no flashes that hurt the eyes of the target are used; these can be obviated on the ground that they cause physical harm to their victims.) The answer is, again, simple: privatize the streets and sidewalks. In that way the "external diseconomy" can be internalized. Some street owners will prohibit all picture-taking on their premises. Others will place no restrictions on this practice. Still others will adopt an intermediate stance, allowing it on some days, at certain hours, but not others. Then, customers will sort themselves out on the basis of these rules, much in the same way the smokers will tend to patronize bars and restaurants that welcome the use of tobacco, while nonsmokers will incline themselves in the direction of health food emporia that do not. Here we see the stark role of private property rights in reducing conflict. Whereas under present institutional arrangements, namely public ownership, there is typically a one-size-fits-all rule. But, we are heterogeneous, not homogeneous, as the dissonance between camera bugs and the camera shy surely attest.

A similar analysis applies to the tension between those who want privacy, and others who wish to spam, or send out junk mail. Those who desire to be left alone are more fortunate in the former case since the web comes with a healthy dose of private property rights. If you do not like how one provider blocks out unwanted messages, usually for a fee, you can offer your business to another. The competition between them tends to ensure high quality and low prices. In the case of snail mail, however, all bets are off. The *public* post office provides one set of rules, and woe to those whose tastes are not satisfied by them.

Suppose A desires privacy and builds a twenty-foot-high fence around his house. B, his neighbor, objects on the ground that this appurtenance blocks his ocean view. Here we have a seeming conflict in rights, anathema to the libertarian law code, which is predicated not on their existence, but upon their resolution.

One way out of this quandary is to compromise, maybe with a ten-foot-high fence? This will not work because A could say he was intending to erect a forty-foot-high barrier and, at twenty feet, is already meeting B halfway. It also fails to determine just who is in the right on this matter. Another solution is for the state to enact a zoning rule establishing maximum height regulations, perhaps at five feet. But the government is an illicit institution, since it is predicated upon initiatory force. Perhaps it could stumble upon the correct answer, but it would certainly not be due to the type of immoral organization it is. And, even if it did, we would still need a criterion with which to judge if it had succeeded or not. Further, this is by way of being yet another unprincipled compromise. It is always possible to ask, at least for those of us who are not legal positivists, "The legislature mandated X, but is it correct?"

From the libertarian perspective, matters are clear. No one can own a view. Period. There is simply no way to homestead any such thing. According to this doctrine, the first man who *saw* the sun, the moon, the stars or the ocean becomes the legitimate owner of these things. Or, if we for some unspecified reason posit that he cannot own these entities themselves, but only his (continued) *view* of them, then any time anyone so much as raises an umbrella that interferes with his sight of these bodies, or whenever an airplane flies overhead to the same effect, his rights will have been violated. Were *anyone else* to gaze upward toward the heavens, he would owe the proprietor of the view of them whatever the latter deigned to charge. Preposterous.

There are also insoluble conflicts set up on the basis of this philosophy. I see the way you comb your hair. Your hairstyle thus becomes part of my view. If I own this view, then I can prevent you from getting a haircut since that would interfere with *my* view of you. In a sense, I then own an aspect of you. But the opposite is true as well. You see me, too. Therefore, you own part of me. So, we each own the other as a partial slave? This is silly, since we can then each order the other not to order ourselves around.

No, A is totally in the right, and B completely in the wrong with regard to the twenty-foot fence. As far as the law should be concerned, A may build a fence to the heavens themselves if he wishes. There are, however, several remedies open to B if he does not want to suffer from being boxed in thus. He can purchase a home in a condominium association, where the rules stipulate fence heights. Or, he can sign a restrictive covenant preventing him and his neighbors from building fences above a certain height. If people value their views, the initial developer of the entire large plot of land can increase profits by selling off each parcel with this contractual limitation as part of the deal. Again, private property rights and the free enterprise system ride to the rescue. It is only in this way that people are enabled to sort themselves out geographically according to, in this case, how they rate the importance of maintaining views, versus retaining privacy behind high walls. The person who wants to sun-bathe in the nude without anyone witnessing this spectacle can build himself a roof garden on the top of the tallest skyscraper in the neighborhood; but then he will just have to deal with planes, helicopters, and neighbors who like to stick mirrors on the top of very large poles, without any help from the legal authorities.

Consider the law case Snyder v. Phelps, brought by Albert Snyder against Fred Phelps. The plaintiff is the father of Corporal Matthew Snyder, killed in battle in Iraq. The defendant is pastor of Westboro Baptist Church, a fundamentalist Christian church which strongly opposes homosexuals, so much so that it runs a website called www.godhatesfags.com and engages in public rallies at the funerals of U.S. soldiers, in order to protest against American toleration of gays. Although this lawsuit has strong free speech elements, it is being brought on privacy grounds (intrusion on rights of seclusion and against publicity the law offers to strictly private gatherings, such as funerals).

How would libertarian law adjudicate such a dispute? Do people who hold funerals (and weddings and other private gatherings) have a right to privacy? No, of course not. Privacy is not a right, it is a privilege. It must be paid for in the free society, just like all other desired goods and services. But, under free enterprise, these benefits would be relatively cheap, as would be the case for all products. And how would this be accomplished? Through private property rights, of course. Funeral (wedding, party, any such gathering) crashers are trespassers, and would be dealt with, rather harshly, under the libertarian legal code. Surely, one of the services offered by private funeral homes and cemeteries would be to offer the bereaved family the privacy they desire. Competition between these firms would allow them to proffer this benefit at a modest, and perhaps even a zero, price. Would this keep away the Fred Phelpses and the Westboro Baptist Churches? Would this allow people to hold funerals in private as they would fervently wish? No, of course not. Detractors can still hold their protest vigils directly outside, on the sidewalk abutting the cemetery. But this is not the fault of the private enterprise system. This lacuna stems from the fact that the market is not ubiquitous enough, far from it. To wit, again, the very streets and sidewalks surrounding the funeral are not private property. If they were, funeral homes and cemeteries in all likelihood would locate in places where the wishes of their customers for privacy were respected by sidewalk and street owners. Possibly, they might even have to pay a premium for this, although this is doubtful. But the bottom line is that those who wish for privacy in these circumstances would be able to attain it.

What of the free speech rights of Fred Phelps and his Westboro Baptist Church? Do not they have a right to publicize their views? Of course they do, but, again, only on their own private property, and/or on land they can rent for this purpose. That is, under laissez faire, they would be free to advertise their philosophy concerning homosexuals or anything else for that matter in newspapers, magazines, and periodicals that are willing to carry their message. They may hire billboards for this purpose. They may continue to operate their politically incorrect website, www.godhatesfags.com. They may even picket on the sidewalks and streets abutting funeral homes, provided it is public property.

In the libertarian society, the rights of each of these contending parties, those who wish to hold funerals in private and those who wish to publicize their critical views, are respected.

Let us now consider various governmental initiatives which either purposefully, or as a happenstance, reduce privacy. For example, governmental social security cards, license cards, tags or plates, identity papers, passports, phone records, intrusive census questions that have nothing to do with enumerating the size of the population for representative purposes, breathalyzers, postal inspection of our mail, border crossing examinations of our persons and property, mobile phone tracking, taping our phone conversations, the governmental release of private information about us, copying our e-mail messages, placing cameras all over the place ostensibly to stop crime and/or traffic violations, breaking and entering into private homes and businesses (with or without warrants) in order to sniff out victimless crimes such as illegal immigration, drug use, homosexuality, etc. Then, there are some of the more exotic programs either already in operation or just over the horizon: a biometric national id card (utilizing pictures of our eye balls and/or the backs of our hands), digital technology to scan our fingerprints, using our genetic codes, placing GPS monitors on our persons, homes, automobiles; last but certainly not least, employing machines that allow minions of the state to see beneath our clothing at airports. Do not these violate our rights to privacy? No, they do not, since we have no right to privacy in the first place. Does the libertarian support any, let alone all, of these programs? No, of course not.

Each and every one of them violates the libertarian legal code, but for different reasons. I don't go so far as to say that every act of government is necessarily illicit from this perspective. Certainly, if we take them out of the context of how they are financed (coercively), when government agents stop a rapist, or rescue someone from a fire, these are legitimate acts. Yet, there is a presumption that each and every deed undertaken by the state is contrary to just law. And this applies, in spades, to its violations of our privacy "rights."

For example, the government compels people to pay for social security, to obtain passports or motor vehicle licenses if we want to travel, to answer census questions. Sometimes, government employs a quid pro quo. We will be allowed to do something, but only if we are willing to give to the state private information about ourselves. For example, we can drive if we obtain a license to do so, which entails that we offer our addresses, dates of birth, etc. Now, there is nothing *per se* wrong with a quid pro quo. All commercial interaction involves just that. (I'll give you something, if you give me something else.)

But the question is, does the government have the *right* to prohibit you from the use of the roads, the borders, the air terminals, the postal service, etc., unless you give it the information it requires? From at least the libertarian point of view, the answer is a very clear no. So, in all such cases, the state's invasion of our privacy is illicit, but *not* because we have rights to privacy. Rather, since they are trading in on a quid pro quo threat they have no right to employ in the first place, for they are not the legitimate owners of these facilities.

Policemen have no right whatsoever to violate our privacy benefits, or privileges, to stop victimless crimes. What of actual crimes such as murder, rape, and assault? May a policeman break into private property with the suspicion that such activities are taking place? Yes, of course. Not government police, which should not exist in the first place, but, certainly, private defenders of law and order. What will happen to them should they do so erroneously is a question too far afield from the concerns of the present chapter—privacy—for a full analysis; suffice it to say that this police company will have to pay the going rate for trespass, just like anyone else. Unless, that is, they have a prior contract with the homeowner which negates this presumption; but, presumably, anyone who wanted his private property protected would be more than willing to enter into such a prior agreement.

According to Constitutional Amendment 4 - Search and Seizure (Ratified 12/15/1791, emphasis added): "The *right* of the people to be secure in their persons, houses, papers, and effects, against unreasonable searches and seizures, shall not be violated, and no Warrants shall issue, but upon probable cause, supported by Oath or affirmation, and particularly describing the place to be searched, and the persons or things to be seized." We have no such *right*. It is merely a privilege, one that, fortunately, the free market system can bestow upon us.

19.

THE AGEIST

King Canute ordered the waves not to come onto the beaches of his empire. In similar fashion, various levels of government are trying to stem the flow of time and aging—by ordering citizens to disregard their effects. Canute failed to flout the laws of nature, and the government is not likely to succeed either.

Consider the following items:

• A mother of a four-year-old girl argues in a Midwestern court that the local school district which admits children only after they have reached their fifth birthday is discriminating.

• A radio station is ordered by a human rights commission to apologize to an eleven-year-old girl for not allowing her to participate in a phone-in show—discussing male strippers— because of her tender years.

• A major air carrier is found guilty of discrimination for its policy of giving special preference to pilot trainees between the ages of twenty-one and twenty-seven.

There is a great difficulty with the position staked out on age by this "human rights" movement. In prohibiting age discrimination, it flies in the face of reality, nature, and common sense—to say nothing of the human right to discriminate on

145

the basis of age. The desire to age discriminate is pervasive, ranging over all sorts of human institutions and endeavors. The cases cited above are only the tip of the iceberg.

People commonly age discriminate in their choice of marital or love partners. The personal advertisements found online and in our newspapers offer ample evidence. "Woman, age ___, seeks man, age ___, object matrimony" is but one example of this. Further, it is the rare client, indeed, who would voluntarily patronize a dentist, attorney, electrician, doctor, plumber, architect or any other such professional, who was six years of age—even if he were a "child prodigy," who had passed all the relevant certification requirements. "Doogie Howser" is of course a counter example, but, remember, this was a *fictional* television program. Nor would it be a popular idea to allow such children to take driver's licensing exams; some might even pass, and then where would we be?

A furniture store in a West Coast city is yet another blatant age discriminator. Its "ballroom," a romper room for children, filled with nothing but styrofoam balls three feet deep, prohibits entry to children under four—a loose, dirty diaper would be a disaster—and over nine—they might frolic too roughly and squash the smaller kiddies.

Don't people have a human right to discriminate in this manner?

So counterintuitive and ridiculous is the prohibition against age discrimination that even the human rights commissions themselves can act sensibly upon occasion when matters of public safety are at issue. But when they do, they must renounce basic tenets of their philosophy.

For example, a human rights commission found that ten airline pilots who were forced to retire at age sixty were *not* victims of age discrimination. It ruled that the airlines were not guilty because forced retirement of airline pilots at age sixty was "normal practice" in the industry.

" I CAN'T TELL YOU HOW DISAPPOINTED I AM,
DOCTOR WHITE, I WAS GIVEN TO UNDERSTAND THAT
THERE'D BE FREE BALLOONS AND LOLLIPOPS AT
THAT EPIDEMIOLOGY SEMINAR IN BOSTON. "

However welcome this decision was on grounds of safety and common sense, it was clearly arbitrary and illogical. If "normal practice" can be a defense against the charge of discrimination, then any discriminator can escape being held culpable as long as there are many others who also follow his practice.

Age is clearly a proxy, or stand in, for other human attributes. It is quick, easy, and inexpensive to determine a person's age, as opposed to tracking and testing mental acuity, reaction times, and skills. If human capacities did not vary with age, there would be little sense in discrimination on this basis, and it is unlikely that it would occur. But abilities do vary with age. The reason we don't send three-year-olds to school, or allow eleven-year-olds to debate the merits or demerits of male strippers, is because such children do not usually have the maturity to be able to handle these experiences. The reason airlines like to train young pilots and retire old ones is that it usually takes a long time to learn the necessary skills which tend to deteriorate as the body's reaction times slow in old age.

There are, of course, exceptions to all such rules of thumb. *Some* three-year-old girls, conceivably, could be trusted to go to school, keep their diapers clean, discuss sexology, get married, drive an automobile or act as a qualified doctor or lawyer. *Some* seventy-five-year-old men might be relied upon to continue to pilot aircraft successfully. And it certainly is "unfair," in at least some sense of that much abused word, to prevent such talented people, if ever they could be found, from taking on these roles.

But the point is, shall such exceptional individuals be allowed to thrust themselves upon an unwilling society? The airline companies are, in the final analysis, only the agents of the flying public. They will not voluntarily employ even an otherwise fully qualified seventy-five-year-old pilot because their *customers* will fear for their lives (however irrationally, in these few exceptional cases). Laws which force over-age pilots upon airlines are ultimately a violation of the human rights of the air passengers, as well as an interference with the airline industry.

20.

THE HOMOPHOBE

In October 1983, an appellate court in Los Angeles ruled that the Boy Scouts of America could not discriminate against homosexual Scout leaders.

This decision was widely hailed as a victory for civil rights by homosexual groups, by "human rights" associations—and by the homosexual Scout leader in question. Said the assistant Scoutmaster one Timothy Curran, "I'm very surprised and pleased with this court decision. I think the Boy Scouts will have a very hard time proving I'm immoral in a trial."

Mr. Curran, who was twenty-one years of age at the time his case was heard, was also a senior majoring in English literature at the University of California at Berkeley. He was the assistant Scoutmaster of Troop 37 of the Mount Diablo council. But he was dismissed from his post when the council learned of his sexual preferences. In the view of the Boy Scout leaders in charge, even though Curran had attained the highest rank of Eagle Scout and was one of the most highly motivated scouts in the organization, a homosexual was not considered a good role model for the young boys in the troop.

Now, there are two schools of thought on the question of discrimination. According to one, that which is beloved of

149

" WATCH NOW, BOYS, THE FRICTION FROM RUBBING
TWO STICKS TOGETHER WILL PRODUCE A SMALL
FLAME AND SOON THESE TWO HOMOPHOBES WILL
BE NOTHING BUT A MEMORY."

the "human rights" activists, discrimination is always and ever wrong, pure and simple. In this view, the California appeals court was quite correct in upholding the right of the homosexual, Timothy Curran, to maintain his position as an assistant scoutmaster. Troop 37 had discriminated against him and had to be stopped from such an egregious practice.

There is a logical difficulty with this view, however. For Curran himself, as a practicing homosexual, discriminates against all women as romantic attachments. The "human rights" movement is logically inconsistent here. It cannot, in the name of supporting anti-discrimination, take the part of a homosexual, a self-confessed discriminator if ever there was one. Rather, if it wished to be logically consistent, this movement should confine itself to championing the rights of bisexuals, people who will form romantic relationships with members of *either* sex. Only they are the true non-discriminators in sexual matters.

But we all discriminate on some grounds. We do so on the basis of honesty or beauty or talent or common interests or what have you. Even bisexuals are guilty of these practices. So it is entirely impossible to consistently adopt a policy of anti-discrimination.

In March 1998, the California Supreme Court reversed the appellate court's decision, ruling that the Boy Scouts has the right to exclude homosexuals from its ranks. Two years later, in June 2000, the U.S. Supreme Court reversed a New Jersey Supreme Court ruling, in a case very similar to Timothy Curran's, that the dismissal of a gay Scout leader had been illegal under the state's anti-discrimination law. This is good news for the Boy Scouts, for if the California appellate court's decision had been upheld at the highest level, the organization would have been doomed. How many heterosexual parents would want to entrust their young boys to the tutelage of homosexual Scout leaders?

A similar situation exists for the Big Brothers of Greater Los Angeles, the organization dedicated to matching fatherless boys with adult males who can guide, counsel, and advise them. At around the same time young Timothy Curran was taking the Boy Scouts to court in Los Angeles, the Big Brothers were named as defendant in a lawsuit filed by the American Civil Liberties Union of Southern California. Their sin against the "human rights" philosophy? They had had the temerity to exclude homosexuals and bisexuals, on the ground that they would be improper role models for young boys. The ACLU sued in order to end an act of blatant discrimination against its client, one Richard Stanley, an avowed bisexual.

Make no mistake about it. If litigants like Mr. Stanley and the ACLU prevail in cases of this kind, it will spell the death knell for groups such as Big Brothers. If these organizations

"FOR PETE'S SAKE, TOM. HERE WE'RE ABOUT TO
GO IN AND DEMAND THAT WE BE ALLOWED TO
SERVE AS 'BIG BROTHERS' TO FATHERLESS BOYS,
AND LOOK AT YOU — SLIP SHOWING, BAGGY NYLONS,
HANGING BRA STRAP..."

can no longer guarantee the female heads of single-parent families that their sons will not be placed in an intimate situation with adult male homosexuals or bisexuals, they will soon enough be unwilling to have anything to do with the program.

But do not homosexual and bisexual men have the "right" not to be discriminated against in this matter? That is, do they not have the "right" to have innocent young boys placed in their tender care, against the wishes of their parents or guardians if need be? Even to ask such a question is to see the utter ludicrousness of it. No one has the "right" to impose himself on an unwilling victim. If anything, the bisexual man has more of a "right" to enter into a dating relationship with the boy's mother, against her will, than into a Big Brother relationship with her son, without her permission. For at least she is an adult; her son is not. And of course, no man, of whatever sexual preference or practice, has a "right" to utilize the law of the land to force a woman to enter into a relationship with him. Even less so, then, can he properly use the courts to become Big Brother to her young son.

And this has nothing to do with the question of whether or not the homosexual or bisexual will use his Big Brother status to seduce the youngster. Rape, and other abuse of position, is certainly not unknown in the heterosexual world. Our conclusion follows solely from the fact that in a free society all relationships should be based on mutual consent. Every person thus has the right to ignore or boycott or discriminate against those whom he would rather avoid. This emphatically includes the many individuals and private organizations, such as the United Way and various corporate and charitable foundations, that have withdrawn their financial support from the Boy Scouts in the wake of the U.S. Supreme Court's ruling. And in turn, those of us who favor the right of the Boy Scouts and other such groups to discriminate against homosexual leaders should be free to boycott the United Way.

In the society we live in, however, our right to discriminate against those we would rather avoid is not protected by government; in fact, one can be punished by the state for exercising that right. If the case of the Salvation Army may be taken as illustrative, one can be punished for far *less* than actually engaging in unlawful discrimination.

The Salvation Army found itself in hot water in New York City. The municipal government was threatening to renege on $5 million dollars worth of contracts already signed with Sally Ann, mainly to manage daycare and senior citizens' centers. The Big Apple's complaint? The Salvation Army had *refused to sign a pledge saying it does not discriminate against homosexuals.*

According to Salvation Army Lieutenant Colonel Roland Schram, his organization did not want to discriminate against homosexuals in its employment practices. However, as a fundamentalist Christian group, it takes a strong pro-family-life position and doesn't want to be seen as—or actually be guilty of—undermining the institution of the family.

But discrimination is discrimination, no matter what the motive in any particular case. And the Salvation Army's hiring practices had run afoul of New York City's Human Rights legislation, which bans discrimination against homosexuals and numerous other groups of people. In the years since, Sally Ann has found herself in similar trouble on the West Coast and elsewhere in the United States. So the real question is: Does the Salvation Army, or anyone else for that matter, have a *right* to discriminate against homosexuals?

If they don't, what becomes of the human right to religious freedom? Do not fundamentalist Christians have the right to practice their calling according to their own principles? The $5 million contract in New York City is only the tip of the iceberg. More to the point, the Salvation Army and other religious groups, such as the Catholic Church and the Orthodox Jews, are guilty of violating the human rights proscription of discrimination against homosexuals in hiring. For none of them will ordain homosexuals as ministers or rabbis. Should the general of the Salvation Army, along with the pope, the cardinals, the bishops and the rabbis, be sent to jail? Hardly. Yet *this* is the logical implication of our extremist, hysterical and ill-founded human rights legislation.

Let us consider one last example of "human rights" riding roughshod over the human right of free association. The online dating service e-Harmony was started in 2000 by Dr. Neil Clark Warren, a clinical psychologist and former dean at Fuller Theological Seminary. He launched this company in an explicit attempt to promote his religious and pro-family philosophy by encouraging marriages for single males and females. In 2008, very much against its will, it agreed to settle a lawsuit brought against it by New Jersey's Civil Rights Division. It did so by launching a new dating website for homosexuals. To add insult to injury, in 2010 it was again forced to undertake another initiative: to bring together under one roof its previously separate heterosexual and homosexual websites and to better promote the latter. We have gone from an era when gays were (totally unjustifiably) brutalized, to one where they had as many rights, no more, no fewer, as anyone else, to the modern epoch where they are allowed to rend asunder the institutions of other people who are themselves innocent of any real crime.

All of this has been accomplished under the banner of nondiscrimination. But this legal philosophy is dead from the neck up. Even its advocates do not take it seriously. If they did, this law would not be applied so haphazardly, and, yes, discriminatorily. For example, if a Chinese restaurant were to ban Jews from entry, this would be summarily brought to a halt by our forces of law and order. If a Jewish eating establishment refused to serve Chinese people, the same fate would befall them. But, if Jewish diners refused to patronize Chinese restaurants, even kosher ones, and Chinese people declined to eat at delicatessens, both sets of vicious and blatant discriminators would escape scot-free from the clutches of our politically correct policemen. Why impose this law on eateries, but not customers?

Similarly, there is simply no justification for imposing these draconian interferences with the right of free association on people in their commercial roles, but not in their private lives. There is simply no case for forcing people to associate with one another against their will in business, but not in other aspects of life. For example, if it is against "human rights" to discriminate against others in hiring, university admissions and "public" accommodation such as restaurants and stores, why not, also, with regard to friendship and marriage? Should we not have compulsory mixed marriages? Of course, no one, that is, *no one*, advocates any such thing, even the most fervent supporters of "human rights." Why ever not, hypocrites?

21.

STEREOTYPER

Stereotypes get bad press in our modern politically correct era. Those who engage in creating and disseminating them are seen as promoting discrimination, profiling, hard feelings, ignorance, and worse.

Yet, stereotypes are no more than broad empirical generalizations; they are based on the valid scientific method of induction. People notice, over and over again, certain broad patterns. Often, these concern characteristics of races, genders, species, animals, minerals, vegetables, etc.; their casual empiricism is so overwhelming that the counter examples are widely seen as the exceptions that prove the rule.

Since stereotypes about human beings come so encumbered with all sorts of negative connotations, let us begin our examination of this phenomenon in calmer terrain. Consider dogs, for example.

Correct stereotypes:

• Alaskan huskies are good at pulling sleds. They are the dog of choice when it comes to the Iditarod. They have thick coats and are impervious to the cold.

• The Bichon Frise is a lap dog and is cuddly and affectionate.

- The Doberman Pinscher is a guard dog that is, loyal, fierce, brave, unafraid, aggressive, and energetic.
- The German Shepherd is, as its name implies, bred to guard sheep.
- The greyhound is very speedy, capable of speeds over 40 miles per hour. It has little body fat and is subject to cold.
- The Chihuahua is very small, can be trained to use a litter box and is temperamental.
- The Saint Bernard is the gentle giant of the dog kingdom.
- The dachshund is the frankfurter dog that tends to dig, and is subject to spinal cord problems.

The above listing and descriptions are all stereotypes. In general, the descriptions are true, but there are exceptions. There is, after all, such a rare thing as a vicious bichon frise and a gentle Doberman. But, by and large, dogs do tend to fall into the described categories.

The "proof" that there is indeed a lot of accuracy in these descriptions is seen when we invert them. Accordingly, the following list of descriptions is generated by applying these descriptions to entirely erroneous subjects.

- The Alaskan husky is the frankfurter dog, tends to dig and is subject to spinal cord problems.
- The bichon frise is a guard dog that is loyal, fierce, brave, unafraid, aggressive, and energetic.
- The Doberman pinscher is a lap dog and is cuddly and affectionate.
- The German shepherd is very speedy, capable of speeds over 40 miles per hour, has little body fat and is subject to cold.
- The greyhound is, as its name implies, bred to guard sheep.
- The Chihuahua is the gentle giant of the dog kingdom.
- The Saint Bernard is very small, can be trained to use a litter box and is temperamental.
- The dachshund is good at pulling sleds and they are the dog of choice when it comes to the Iditarod. They have thick coats and are impervious to the cold.

The above, inverted list is just plain silly. If read while under the influence of your drug of choice, it can even be funny, offering proof to the claim that there was more than just a modicum of truth in the original listing. (By the way, there is now a concerted effort to ban Pit Bulls, since a few of them have hurt and even killed some people. But, this is equivalent to "dog profiling.")

Having established this principle with regard to dogs, let us try it out on human beings, based on race, nationality, gender.

Correct stereotypes:

• Jews are very smart and studious. They have made marks in business, science, law, and medicine. They have a deserved reputation for driving hard bargains. They suffer more than most from Tay-Sachs disease.

• Italians love opera and spaghetti. Emotionally expressive, they are noted for contributions to the arts, leather goods, and wine making.

• Irish believe in leprechauns. Their drug of choice is liquor. They are feisty and argumentative.

• Swedes are morose and taciturn. Fair-skinned with blond hair and blue eyes, they have high rates of suicide.

• The French are the greatest cooks in the world. They are expert wine connoisseurs.

• Blacks are great athletes, particularly in basketball, track, and football. They are also well-noted as musicians, particularly in jazz, hip hop, and rap. They are statistically over proportionally represented among criminal classes. They suffer from sickle cell anemia.

• Hispanics are noted for their wonderful ability as dancers.

• Women are nurturing and forge strong bonds with their children. They are given to bouts of hysteria, especially when it is their time of the month.

• Men are aggressive and do not live as long as women. Brave, courageous, risk takers, they are territorial and possessive. They are also more accident prone than women.

To say that the stereotyper has had a bad press of late is the understatement of the year. He is utterly reviled on all fronts. Stereotyping is politically incorrect. It is dismissed as the vilest of prejudices. Surely, no one, apart from a few red-neck southerners or members of the Ku Klux Klan with Nazi affiliations would engage in so despicable an act. The latter are stereotypes too, of course, but they are acceptable in polite company since it is politically correct to pillory such groups, just not hippies, union members or Communists.

Not so fast. Let us take a deep breath and reflect upon what, precisely, it is of which the stereotyper is guilty. What is stereotyping? It is no more and no less than generalizing on the basis of past evidence. It amounts to prejudging this one particular instance on the basis of previous observations that resemble this one. (Prejudice, the act of prejudging, has also come in for its fair share and more of opprobrium. We defend this practice, too, in the present chapter.)

Let's look at that old saying, "I'm firm, you're stubborn and he's a pig-headed fool." Emotively, these are very different characterizations; the first is a strong positive, the second a moderate negative, and the third a downright slur. And, yet, substantively, they indicate a person who sticks to his principles, who the speaker supports, or slightly or heavily condemns, respectively. In a similar manner, we could say with regard to stereotyping that I am scientific and rely on induction, you, a mere pragmatist, are swayed by public opinion; he, on the other hand, is a prejudiced stereotyper. Again, the first of these is a compliment, the second somewhat of a criticism (at least in non-pragmatic circles), and the third one of the worst appellations anyone can hurl at anyone else. And yet, the thesis of the present chapter is that when it comes to substance, there is as little difference between the latter set of three descriptions (concerning stereotyping) as there is in the former case (regarding firmness of belief).

What, then, is induction? It is, along with deduction, one of the two pillars of the scientific method. Induction is the drawing of conclusions from past experience, from observations or experiments. For example, here is knowledge attained from induction: one part oxygen and two parts hydrogen combine to create water; black athletes make superlative basketball players; whites are good swimmers; the sun will rise tomorrow. We learn these truths merely by inspection of the real world. In deduction, in contrast, we reach conclusions not from experience, but based on pure logic. For example, we know that if all men are mortal, and if Socrates is a man, then he is mortal. This follows merely, and entirely, from pure reason; we do not, and, indeed, cannot, experience any of this. In contrast, there is no necessity that H20 yield water, that blacks be good at dunking the basketball, that whites win swimming medals, that the next day will dawn. Things could have been different. In an alternative universe, whatever that may mean, these facts might well be otherwise. At least we can *imagine* a world where these statements are not true. In sharp contrast, there are no exceptions in matters of logic. In *all* cases where A>B>C, it follows that A>C; there is simply no getting around the fact that if all men are mortal and Socrates is a man, then Socrates is mortal. This is true in any universe. With empirical generalizations, however, there are often exceptions. These "prove" the rule. Certainly, not all blacks are good hoopsters, let alone excellent ones. Some Orientals are good hoopsters; look at Yao Ming.

Let us consider the following stereotypes:
- British are good managers
- Swedes are taciturn
- French are good cooks
- Irish are happy-go-lucky
- Blacks are excellent athletes
- Jews are smart
- Asians are math whizzes

- Italians are great lovers
- Men are taller than women

These are all empirical generalizations. They are judgments made on the basis of vast experience of millions of people over many years. Are these claims without exception? Of course not. Some Swedes are ebullient; some Orientals cannot add 2+2 and arrive at 4. (I have never met any such mathematically challenged Asians above the age of 18 months, but I'm sure there are some.) Certainly, not all men are taller than all women. But, are these *correct* generalizations? Are they broadly based empirical realities? Of course they are. They would hardly rise to the level of stereotypes were they not.

One way to demonstrate this is to invert them. That is, instead of correctly attributing characteristics to ethnic and racial groups, we purposefully do the very opposite. Consider then, the following false stereotypes.

- Italians are good managers
- Eskimos are world class soccer players
- British are happy-go-lucky
- Jews are drunken brawlers
- Blacks are math whizzes
- Irish are the best basketball players
- French are taciturn
- Orientals dominate the NFL
- Italians always win the Iditarod
- Women are taller than men

These are not only false, some of them are ludicrous. Thus, we can see that by inverting stereotypes and reaching obviously silly conclusions, we must all the more support the original list of generalizations gained from hard-won experience.

A friend and onetime co-author of mine tells the following story: He will offer some opponent of stereotypes one hundred dollars to go to an unfamiliar college campus and choose two students, one of whom can dunk a basketball, the other who can solve a quadratic equation. Should you choose a tall, black young man (heck, even a short one) for the first task and a small Asian student with eyeglasses as thick as the bottom of a Coca Cola bottle for the second, or should you reverse this? Recourse to the relevant stereotypes is obviously the most likely way to earn this one hundred dollars. There are no guarantees, of course. This choice will not necessarily bring home the bacon. But it is more likely, *far* more likely, to do so.

Why is this the case? In a word, prejudice. Or more accurately, or etymologically correct, pre-judice. You are pre-judging the two students and their capacities if you make the decision likely to win you that one hundred dollars. On what basis are you selecting these two students? Why, it is due to a plethora of previous experience. You know, also, that the Asian student is far more likely to know how to do a karate kata and bow away on the violin, whereas the young black man is more likely to shoot hoops and play the saxophone.

Suppose you open the door to your living room and see a tiger sitting on your couch. Would you, you prejudiced stereotyper, immediately close the door, lock it and call the police, or, would you spurn such politically incorrect prejudiced stereotypical behavior, and, check things out with an open mind? If the latter, you would enter the living room, maybe allow the tiger to sniff your fist, maybe try to pat it to show you are friendly and then find out if *this particular* tiger will eat you for breakfast. You know that, as a general rule, tigers are inclined to munch first and ask questions later, but you don't want to be a prejudiced stereotyper (I can't help it, I love that phrase; it is the essence of political incorrectness; it packs into a mere two words so much that left liberals find despicable), so you are willing to ignore such findings from past experience. But, if you had even the barest modicum of good sense, you would be pre-judging this particular tiger, about which you have absolutely no knowledge, based on the behavior you (and many others) have seen *other* tigers exhibit in the past. You would tend to live longer, too, if you embraced your inner stereotyper.

But isn't this unfair? Surely, *this* tiger should not be painted with the brush depicting other vicious animals of this species. *This* tiger, we may suppose, arguendo, has never so much as hurt a fly. All I can say about this is, tough cookies about your hurt feelings, tiger; prejudice and stereotyping über alles.

Given that pre-judging, stereotyping and inferring from past to future experience is so eminently reasonable, so scientific, in that it utilizes induction, why the calumny heaped upon those who engage in such behavior?

This can only be speculative, but one of the reasons might well be the political correctness that has swept campus, pulpit and newsroom of late. This has made it an act of courage to even utter words like Miss, Mrs., black, prejudice, stereotyping, Oriental, Negroid, white, African-American, and a whole host of others.

And why, pray tell, would the forces of political correctness fasten on prejudice and stereotyping with particular venom? They are part and parcel of sometimes invidious comparisons made by social scientists and the man in the street (to employ yet another verboten phrase). The forces of political correctness no doubt think it unfair if lowered expectations, due to stereotyping, lead to lesser performance than would otherwise be the case. For example, if it is noted that blacks are not good swimmers, this will decrease their times in the 100 meter butterfly; if white men are told they cannot jump well, this will reduce their self esteem, and their hang times will be reduced even more. But it has by no means been proven that expertise and success is a function of expectations, of oneself or of others. In any case, possibly, half of stereotypes are *positive*. Was Usain Bolt's smashing of the world's records in the 100- and 200-yard dash really due to positive stereotypes about black runners? If so, why don't *all* members of this race continually emulate him in these Herculean records? If Keynesian "animal spirits" are the best explanation of economic success, and they can be engendered by stereotypes, they ought to balance each other out on this basis.

Another reason for the common rejection of stereotypes is that intellectual elites are too "cosmopolitan" to appreciate them. These leaders have a strong inclination toward egalitarianism. But stereotypes make what they see as invidious comparisons between groups. Now, no one class of people can outperform any other in every capacity. Thus, no one race or ethnic group can be "better" than any other. But some peoples lose out in competition with others in terms of particular characteristics deemed important. This, the modern fetish of egalitarianism cannot tolerate. Hence, their bitter rejection of all things smacking of stereotyping.

Let us close by asking, why is it that stereotypes are invariably *true*? Why don't the false stereotypes mentioned above (whether for dogs or humans) ever arise and gain currency? This is because of mankind's basic common sense. If a person continually promoted false pre-judices (Eskimos are excellent camel racers; Arabs are masters of the snow environment) he would be laughed at by all and sundry. Actually believing in such utter nonsense, moreover, could not have strong survival values.

According to encyclopedia.com, stereotyping amounts to:

"Making assumptions about individuals or groups based on information (which may or may not be valid) obtained before the individual or group has been encountered. Once encountered, opinions formed may be based on dress, speech, gender, ethnic origin, nationality, and gestures. Unfortunately, human beings are liable to have selective prejudices towards their fellows, seeing only what they want to see and ignoring factors that do not fit in with their preconceived beliefs. They also tend to assume that all the individuals of a group have the same, or similar, characteristics. Thus: all graduates are clever; all unemployed people are lazy; are two of the stereotypes that have to be resisted in carrying out job selection interviews."

But this is obviously a biased and erroneous understanding of the concept. *Of course* it is not true that *all* graduates are clever, or that *all* unemployed people are lazy. But, what of the more moderate and reasonable interpretation of these stereotypes: that graduates are, *on average*, more clever than non-graduates, or that the unemployed are lazier, *in the main*, than the employed. These latter claims may or may not be true at all times and at all places, but they are at least not straw men. Indeed, if all you knew about a person was that he was a graduate (non-graduate), or employed (unemployed), you would be entitled to draw *some* conclusions from this information. The critics of stereotyping would deny this. Let us resort to our above-mentioned technique for dealing with these issues; stereotypical inversion.

Thus, we ask, not which set of statements is *necessarily* true, but which is *more likely* to be the case.

A: all graduates are clever; all unemployed people are lazy

B: all *non*-graduates are clever; all *employed* people are lazy

Placing matters in this manner indicates the utter foolishness of the dictionary author's claim. A is presumptively true; B is just plain silly. How can it *be* that all *employed* people are lazy? They are *working*, are they not? As such, they have at least one very important advantage over the unemployed in the non-laziness sweepstakes: they are *employed*, for goodness sakes, and, other things equal, people who are working are presumably less lazy than those who are not. Similar remarks apply to the issue of cleverness. If the graduates are so stupid, how in bloody blue blazes did they *graduate*? I know, I know, given the forces of political correctness nowadays rampant everywhere, but particularly on our nation's campuses, merely passing all courses in a four-year program means very little. But, it still means *something*. At the very least, a student has to master (if I can still use that word?) subjects such as mathematics, chemistry, etc., that the feminist and multicultural forces have not yet been able to pervert. And, too, one must exhibit, at least, a certain low cunning to not violate the often confusing strictures of political correctness.

VI. BUSINESS

22.

THE WAR TOY MANUFACTURER

What do some peace groups, religious organizations, feminists, and child care experts have in common? They are up in arms (pardon the pun) against war toys.

The Council of Churches has published a brochure urging the creation of "war-toy-free zones." The Mennonite Central Committee has organized a letter-writing campaign to protest against firms manufacturing these playthings. The Voice of Women and the Alliance for Non-Violent Action have attempted to organize a consumer boycott of war toys. Parents for Peace conducts study groups on the topic of war toys, publishes a list of alternative toys, and creates strategies for parents whose children demand war toys instead of the recommended alternatives. Child care expert Benjamin Spock, author of *Baby and Child Care*, which has sold more than thirty million copies since 1946, was a leader of this protest as well. In his view, "when we buy (children) machine guns and bombs and helmets and encourage them to play war, we are saying to them that war is all right." The Alliance for Non-Violent Action, in addition to conducting a boycott of the non-toy products of war toy manufacturers, has initiated the first International

Day Against War Toys complete with vigils, leaflets, and a door-to-door campaign. In the most bizarre incident of all, the top editors of the magnificent libertarian website antiwar.com, railed against J. C. Penney for daring to market a war toy called Forward Command Post. (See http://www.antiwar.com/ comment/jcpenney.html and http://www.antiwar.com/justin/j122502.html.) These critics make the point that Forward Command Post (FCP) depicts a middle-class home in the U.S., not a foreign country, and that seems "sinister" to them. Well, maybe it is; I respect the radar of these writers. But, this game is for *five year olds*. It is greatly to be doubted that any of these tykes would see the FCP scenario in the very sophisticated manner of the antiwar.com analysts.

Whatever the merits of their case, it is clear that these groups and individuals have their work cut out for them. No longer is it a simple matter of fighting off only the G.I. Joe dolls. (The Council of Churches advocated that these be redesigned as the "Builder Joes, Creators of the Universe.") Nowadays, the protest movement must fend off such creations as toy Uzis, M-16s, submarine super pistols, lasers, Luger P-128s, and a horde of armed-to-the-teeth robots, gobots, transformers, inceptors, Star Wars animals, He-Men, She-Ras, and so on. A few decades ago, the Rambo insignia was brought to market on at least seventy separate items, including pajamas, bubble gum, watches, and flashlights. And in the years since, violent, war-centered video games, the brain children of computer geniuses like Nolan Bushnell (Atari) and John Carmack (the man behind Doom) have been making news and spurring commentary and denunciations.

High tech has long been a part of the war toy scene. The Tech Force robots, for example, could be remote controlled, said Newsweek, "by audio signals encoded in the sound tracks of television programs or video cassettes. A child will be able to pit a robot he is controlling against one responding to TV signals. The robots, six to eight inches tall, will move, make sound and fire infrared beams at each other on command; a direct hit will temporarily disable the enemy robot."

Let us move on from the toys and the protesters and look at the arguments put forth by each side to the controversy.

Exhibit "A" in the case against war toys is the view that they desensitize children to war. In a nuclear era, it is particularly important not to pass on warlike values, is the contention made by the protesters.

But there are several objections to be made. First, there is no hard and fast evidence linking war toys for children to warlike behavior as adults. War toys so permeate our society that it would be difficult to even imagine finding subjects upon whom truly double blind longitudinal experiments could be performed. The Board of Education of a major city studied the incidence of violence and the macabre in student essays from grades four to seven, and concluded that these graphic depictions of bloodshed and murder were "often influenced by violence in television and movies." But there are numerous objections to this interpretation. Other sources of this behavior were not ruled out. It was not a longitudinal study; no adult warlike activities were thereby explained. If true, however, this is actually evidence against the thesis that war *toys* help foment war; for we now have an alternative hypothesis: violent *movies* do so.

Secondly, there is the argument that some measure of desensitization greater than zero is optimal. War, after all, is a grisly business, but there are defensive and therefore justified wars. Even if war toys do indeed desensitize what would otherwise be "natural" anti-war feelings, they may still be appropriate. An alternative explanation is that toy guns have little to do with war in the minds of children, but much to do with good against evil.

A third objection is that if war toys are banned, children may possibly remain unprepared for real life, which does contain an aspect of violence, even in modern, supposedly civilized times.

War toys, in this analysis, are simply a means of preparing children for adulthood.

A second arrow in the quiver of the protest faction is the idea that dolls like G. I. Joe, with their predefined roles of good and bad guys, inhibit creativity. According to one childhood education specialist, "Before (war toy) marketing, children were free to play in their own way. But now a child does not have to build his own structures." This claim, too, must be taken with a grain of salt, as there is no independent verification of it. As well, most creative men played with guns when they were boys. This hardly amounts to a controlled experiment, but it would appear to be a common sense refutation of the idea that war toys stifle creativity. Rather, in the view of many adult males, the protest amounts to little more than a sort of feminist plot to turn little boys into wimps. However, given the argument from ignorance (e.g., that there are so many other toys for children to play with, why choose the debatable ones) it may be the better part of valor for parents to go along with the boycott.

The defenders of war toys are not without a defense of their own, however. One argument put forth is that these playthings are a positive way for youngsters to channel their aggressions. If so, war toys ought to be negatively correlated with the incidence of juvenile delinquency—another untested, not to say untestable, proposition.

This view, however, has not gone uncriticized. According to one author, if war toys prevent or at least lessen aggressive impulses, then why not advocate "break and enter" kits to reduce criminality, or, as one columnist suggested not long ago, "Kids' Fix Kits," which would include "a small plastic hypodermic needle, a piece of rubber tube, and a little spoon and candle" in order to decrease drug addiction?

This, it must be admitted, is a very clever attempt at a *reductio ad absurdum*, but ultimately it fails. This is because it does not logically follow that just because a "B & E Kit" will

"A GROUP CAME IN TO PICKET THE WAR TOYS AND WHEN THEY SAW THAT SIGN I PUT UP, THEY QUIETLY LEFT."

not diminish juvenile delinquency, or a "Kids' Fix Kit" retard drug addiction rates, that war toys cannot reduce aggression. Conceivably, they can; whether they do or not is a so-far undetermined empirical question not answerable by resort to *reductio ad absurdum*, no matter how clever. The analogy between these three types of activities is also somewhat suspect. Little *children*, especially boys, like to say "bang, bang" while pointing their fingers in the form of a gun. They do this practically from the age at which they can first speak— but small tots typically don't play B & E games, or "shoot up" anything into their veins, even when given doctor sets.

Having discussed the pros and cons, then, how can we evaluate the case put forth by each side? This all depends upon the type of analysis we are considering. If we are giving advice to parents, who want to bring up their children as best they can, we must unfortunately leave them to their own devices. This is because, while there is quite a lot of heat shed by both parties to the dispute, there is little light, in the form of hard evidence. And for the same reason, we cannot determine if it is in the interests of children that war toys be boycotted. People have the right to buy whatever products they wish in a free society; whether it is *wise* to do so in any particular case is an entirely different manner. But it cannot be overly emphasized that those who wish to boycott war toys have a perfect right to do so in a free society—even if it can't be proven, somehow, that these implements are harmful to children. This right flows solely from the law of free association (we all have the right to engage in commercial or any other voluntary interaction with other people solely at our own discretion). It is not at all based on the wisdom or the efficacy of the actions undertaken.

There is, however, an entirely different perspective from which this debate can be approached. We can ask not if it is *wise* to boycott war toys, but if it is *justified* that war toys be prohibited by legislative enactment.

It might be thought that such a question could have only theoretical interest, because no one has gone so far as to call for the legal prohibition of war toys. That, unfortunately, is not the case. According to one advocate of this very position, "It is dreadful to leave our children's needs to the marketplace." And both consumer groups and church councils have already petitioned government to prohibit TV commercials for war toys, and also violent cartoon shows featuring such weapons.

This disquieting development is certainly an attack on the free speech rights of toy purveyors. Were it not for the fact that children are involved as the ultimate consumers, the case for overriding the marketplace by banning such advertising would be far weaker than it is. But children are involved here.

We must thus face head-on the challenge that these interferences may be justified by that fact.

The case seems strong when we pit the intelligence of the adult would-be regulators against that of the toy users. But bureaucrat jokes about intelligence aside, it must be readily admitted that the toy banners are adults, and the children are not. Thus, in any dispute between them, the presumption is that the views of the former must prevail over those of the latter.

But this is only a presumption. Taken too much to heart, it leads inexorably to a certain view of justice, according to which the faculty of Harvard University should be able to bend other people to its will, for based on many conventional definitions of the phenomenon, the members of the faculty are more intelligent than most other people. But it would be rather difficult to prove that the more intelligent have a right to rule over the rest of us.

The case for banning war toys unravels further when we realize that it is not adult (presumably intelligent) bureaucrats ranged against mere children with too little experience of the world to be able to choose wisely for themselves. On the contrary, it is the parents of these "helpless" children versus the do-gooders. The argument for prohibition fails, even on merely utilitarian grounds, unless it can be shown that in general the state has a better interest in the children than do the parents themselves. Given the lack of evidence one way or another, this would appear to be an insuperable barrier against a legal prohibition.

We must conclude that despite the possible dangers of war toys, there is no case for banning them through legislative enactment. Further, these manufacturers, in having the courage to persevere in their course of action, despite all the calumny foisted upon them, deserve the characterization "heroic."

23.

THE COLORIZER

Colorization has taken our society by storm. This process, which re-issues in color the older black-and-white movie classics such as *Citizen Kane* or *City Lights*, has been greeted with howls of outrage by the arts community. Even though TV watchers can simply dial out the color and view these movies in their original, pristine black and white, the culture vultures are still vociferously opposed.

What is their argument? First of all, there is the claim that these films are part of a "landmark heritage" and any tampering with them is akin to sacrilege. This is a very peculiar view to be put forth by people who are not known for their innate conservatism. Apart from the hypocrisy thus involved, the difficulty with the "whatever is, is right" philosophy is that it is simply not true. Things *can* be improved, the protestations of the recent converts to stick-in-the-mudism notwithstanding.

Nor is it even true that the precious artistic inheritance of black and white will be lost forever. On the contrary, there are *several* copies of these old films in the vaults, and the colorizers always leave a few untouched. The argument on the basis of heritage is specious. It is not that the vintage editions will disappear, merely that they will not be exhibited as widely.

And why should they be, given the preference of a new generation of viewers for color?

One might wince at the prospect of the Mona Lisa being "recolored." It might appear on the same level as drawing graffiti on the picture, or adding a moustache. The integrity of the object would disappear. However, there is a huge difference between the cinema and the great works of art. In the former case, there are several indistinguishable originals; in the latter, there is only one.

Then, there are complaints about the quality of the colorization, and charges that the decision as to which hue shall be used in what places is being made by "unqualified" computer technicians. This argument, too, is erroneous, for the market will tend to insure that only the most gifted colorists will be allowed to touch these precious motion pictures. As well, what we now have before us is the product of a revolutionary process. In time, with technological breakthroughs, we can expect vast improvements.

But the major complaint about the colorizer is that he rides roughshod over the rights of the artist. Says Woody Allen in this regard, "No one should be able to alter an artist's work in any way whatsoever, for any reason, without the artist's consent. It's really as simple as that." There is, however, an obvious retort; these films are not *owned* by the artists who created them. On the contrary, they are the property of those who took the up-front risks of financing them. The point is that when the artist agreed not to become the residual income claimant, i.e., the property owner, but instead to work for him for a fixed fee, he in effect consented to the right of the latter to alter the product.

What is really at stake here is an attempt to satisfy or ignore the wishes of the consumer. This is clear when we ask, "Why is it that the colorizer is attempting to improve these old motion pictures? Is it out of a destructive impulse? Is it because he enjoys ruining the work of artists, better men than he?" Not

"FRANK, I'VE GOT A SCENE WHERE CLARK GABLE IS TALKING HIMSELF 'BLUE IN THE FACE' TO JEAN HARLOW—D'YA THINK CERULEUM IS STRONG ENOUGH?"

a bit of it. It is solely because in attempting to maximize profits, he is led, as if by an "invisible hand," to produce that which will best satisfy the customer.

And the motives of the colorizer's antagonists are equally clear: contempt for the wishes and desires of the public. For example, states Mr. Allen, one of the chief critics, "Nor would I want to see my film *Manhattan* in color. Not if it would bring in ten times the revenue. Not if all the audiences in the world begged or demanded to see it that way." Now, of course, as the owner of this particular movie, he has the complete and absolute right to make this decision. (This statement is subject to qualifications made in the chapter on intellectual property.)

Were he only the artist, and not both the artist and the owner, he would not.

Complains Woody Allen, "In our society, merchants are willing to degrade anything or anyone so long as it brings in a financial profit." The answer to this charge is that artists have the right to try and amass the resources necessary for the creation of a motion picture. If they succeed, then they, as owners, have the right to determine matters such as colorization. But if they do not or cannot, they must be bound by the contract they have signed, which gives these ownership rights to other people.

The merchant in this case is not degrading anything or anyone. He is merely allocating resources in such a way as to maximize consumer satisfaction. This is both the beauty of the free enterprise system and one of its most noble aspects.

24.

THE BABY SELLER

At first blush, there could be fewer things more heinous than child selling. The very concept evokes pictures of child abuse, venality, and greed. Since toddlers are among the most helpless of human beings, our hearts go out to the supposed victims of child selling, and we become enraged at those who perpetrate such a despicable act.

But a moment's reflection will convince us that the word picture offered above is erroneous. For child selling is no more than child *adoption*; only in the latter case no money or other valuable consideration changes hands, while in the former it does.

Certainly, no one opposes a couple adopting a baby who is abandoned, or whose parents can no longer care for him. Provided it is done with proper safeguards to deal with the possibility of child abuse, and assuming no intentions other than bringing up a happy and healthy tyke, there is nothing at all problematic about adoption. Our movie stars are forever going to South America or Africa for this purpose, and no one, except for maybe a few late-night television comedians, casti- gate them for this. Indeed, it is an entirely virtuous act; even if the motives behind it might sometimes be less than fully pure (e.g., personal aggrandizement, publicity), provided that the toddlers are cared for and brought up with love and affection.

But, if X is virtuous, why does it become contemptible just because money changes hands? If it is a good deed to adopt a toddler, why is it illegal to do so when the natural parents are paid to give up their progeny (or, in some case, if the parents pay those who adopt their children)? If it is licit to wash a car, should it be against the law to pay someone to do this (be paid by someone for this purpose)? Given that it is legal to wear a propeller beanie hat on your head, it would be a moral monstrosity to incarcerate someone for "crime" of engaging in such an act under the marketplace or cash nexus.

Yes, yes, babies for sale may be associated with child abuse. It may well even be the case that when the right to bring up a baby is sold, the child is likely to be treated poorly, while in contrast, when the adoption takes place with no money changing hands, the baby's welfare is much improved. I am unaware of any evidence to support this contention, nor is any likely to be found, since adoption for money is illegal. But, let us stipulate that this is true: When adoptions are handled in the marketplace, there are more likely to be abuses than when cash considerations play no role in the proceedings.

So, should we now prohibit an act just because it is statistically correlated with evil and obnoxious behavior? Of course not. If we did, we would immediately prohibit, as a crime, the "act" of being a teenage male. We should lock up all boys as they turn 13, for the "crime" of being a male teen, and then let them go free when they no longer exhibit this "evil" characteristic, namely, upon their 20th birthdays. Why? Because there is a positive statistical correlation between taking on these characteristics, and being guilty of murder, rape, theft, drag racing which eventuates in vehicular manslaughter, etc.

Perhaps clarity might be shed on this entire unhappy legal episode merely by a change in nomenclature. At present, the illegal act, and the title of this chapter is, "baby selling." This, it must readily be admitted, sounds horrible. In contrast, did we but call it "adoption selling," a good bit of the venom might be banished. No one wants to eat "cow flesh" whereas we are all (well, most of us) entirely willing to consume hamburgers, steak, etc. Perhaps, had we been calling them "cow-flesh burgers" they would have been, by now, outlawed. Then, through mere verbal legerdemain, we could end the prohibition of these fast-food items.

But this tells only part of the story. There is a visceral hatred of the market that burns fiercely in the hearts of socialist, fascist, and other interventionistic ideologues. They will not accept what they would undoubtedly interpret as a cheap trick: the alteration from "baby selling" to "sale of adoption rights." Nor is this loathing confined to professional demagogues. It has seeped out, with a vengeance, to the general community. Until and unless this irrational fear and loathing for the free enterprise system can somehow atrophy (the present book is one of many that attempts to move us in this direction), we will continue to suffer from this type of unjust governmental interference with markets.

Money oils the wheels of commerce. When commercial activity is prohibited as in the present case, there are unrequited buyers and sellers who cannot interact with one another for the purpose of mutual gain. To wit, in this case, under present institutional arrangements, there will be some transfers of guardianship rights over kiddies from some parents who value them less, to other potential parents who would value them more, that will not take place. (Who is likely to be the better caretaker of the children: natural parents willing to sell adoption rights, or those who value the children enough to pay for the rights to care for them?) Only that subset of all such transfers will occur that can be accomplished without the intermediation of money. The *children* will suffer as a result of this pernicious law.

25.

HERITAGE BUILDING DESTROYER

There is a small but highly organized and influential group of people who are trying to force their views on aesthetics and history down the throats of the rest of us—whether we like it or not.

I refer to those vociferous busybodies who try to impose historical landmark status on old and decaying buildings in the central city.

These people are usually highly educated, sophisticated, and cultured. They want to indulge their own tastes, and protect the older buildings that people of that ilk enjoy. But this is at the expense of those who might benefit from the jobs and homes that could be created if modern office towers or large apartment blocks were erected on those sites instead.

If these busybodies want to save the buildings they admire, well and good. Let them buy these heritage structures themselves—just as they purchase their antique furniture and vintage cars. But it is entirely unfair to force other people, many of them poorer, to pay for this particular enjoyment of theirs.

Actually, leaving the preservation of heritage buildings up to the marketplace and the price system, rather than forcing the poor to pay for it through government action, might well have a result far better than the one the vociferous busybodies say they expect. For, although it is not widely realized, the price system tends to promote optimal preservation of past relics, as it does of everything else.

Consider the situation with regard to antique furniture. If too few of these relics from the past had been saved, the price system could be counted upon to remedy this situation. Extremely high prices would encourage people to forage around in dumps, etc., in hopes of uncovering more marketable antiques, hence meeting the great demand. The movement would be toward discovery and increased supply.

But it is no less true that an oversupply of artifacts would also create problems. If our homes were too burdened with antiques, then there would be less room for the modern conveniences we also enjoy. If such a situation were somehow to arise, many antiques would lose value and would be summarily destroyed.

Neither of these scenarios is remotely likely, of course. Indeed, the proof that the price system is working well is that both are ludicrous: there is no antique "problem," at least with regard to furniture or automobiles. We have no noticeable over- or under-supply.

Things are entirely different, however, with regard to historical monuments and buildings. The market has all but been banished, and governmental zoning has instead held sway. Consequently, there are indeed serious problems.

Were a price system fully in effect for time-honored buildings, with no zoning interferences, some of them, those worth more *in situ* than demolished, would be preserved. But without a market, the costs of maintaining such structures in pristine condition are ignored. There is no way of telling which are worth more as is, and which are more valuable for the space they release for new construction.

Why would the owner of an antique building preserve it, when he could sell it for millions to a developer? Given that this particular edifice is one that deserves preservation, consumers must value it more for its historical character than for the space it could cede to a skyscraper. (I assume away the possibility of moving the entire building to a different site as too costly.) If so, then the revenue the owner could extract via admission charges, plus his own psychic enjoyment, should more than offset alternative revenues.

Why are so few historical buildings preserved on the market? For one thing, costs are relevant to present economic decision making. This explains why small relics from the past have a greater chance of being preserved, other things being equal, than larger ones. Old stamps and coins, jewelry and children's toys can be preserved at less cost than can automobiles, locomotives, sailing ships, and buildings. Consequently, unless the larger artifacts are more valuable in proportion to the cubic space they occupy (abstracting from additional maintenance costs), fewer of them will be saved for posterity.

But there is another difficulty posed for a market solution to the historic building question: externalities. Before we deal with objections based on this concept, let us offer a scorecard, so that we can tell one ball player, so to speak, from another. Externalities are costs or benefits undertaken by one economic actor, call him A, that spill over onto, or affect, another market participant, call him B. For example, A takes a shower, or washes his car, or trims his lawn. This makes A's neighbor's B's life more enjoyable, and increases the value of B's home. A may have undertaken his actions solely to suit himself, but this has repercussions on B's welfare. So much for positive externalities, or external economies. Now, consider negative externalities, or external diseconomies. A likes to play his stereo, loudly, at 3 a.m. and burns his garbage, right next door to B. A need not intend to impose any costs on B. And if B is deaf and doesn't care about smoke particles invading his lungs, A will not have done so. But, in the more ordinary case, we say that A has indeed imposed costs, some physical, some pecuniary, on B. What most economists make of all this is that the government should subsidize external economies, sometimes called neighborhood effects, and tax or prohibit external diseconomies. For the Austro-libertarian, in sharp contrast, positive externalities are the earmark of civilization, and there is no warrant for government interfering with this boon which is *not* a market failure, at all. As for negative externalities, these, too, do not constitute a market failure. Rather, they are a violation of property rights, and courts should deal with them. With this introduction to these concepts, let us return to the subject at hand.

There may not be any feasible way for consumers to see the inside of the building without paying for the privilege, but the main attraction may be the facade, and all passers-by can enjoy this without charge. How could an entrepreneur internalize this externality and convert the outside of the building into a paying proposition?

The problem arises because not all elements of the situation are part of the competitive market. The streets are government controlled, for example. If they were privately owned, one significant aspect of the externality problem would disappear. The owners of the historic building and of the surrounding streets and sidewalks would presumably come to some agreement concerning the sharing of the revenues collected from the passers-by. Possibly one would buy the other out.

There would remain the question of the surrounding skyscrapers, however. Their owners might well charge admission to their windows or roofs for the purpose of viewing the neighboring attraction. This, of course, could severely hamper the monument owner's efforts to maintain his building as a paying proposition.

But there are several countermeasures he could adopt. He could erect (or threaten to do so) a large fence around the building to cut off a view from the lower floors of neighboring buildings; or a large shield above the roof so that no one on the upper stories of those buildings could enjoy the vista either. Given these possibilities, the surrounding skyscraper owners might be willing to negotiate a payment for the viewing rights. Alternatively, the historic and surrounding structures might come under the same ownership—from one landlord selling to the other, or both to a third party. In any of these eventualities, the externalities would be no more; they would be internalized. The facade of the building, as well as the inside, would be brought into the economic nexus.

Both could be charged for, thus allowing people to register the importance they place upon historicity. The antique monument would remain so, as long as the market value of remaining so continued to be greater than any alternative use of the property. In other words, there is indeed such a thing as *private* zoning. This process need not at all be a monopoly of government.

It is important to realize, however, that not all external benefits need to be internalized. Many, if not most, viable commercial establishments release external benefits for which they are unable to collect. Many people benefit merely from knowing about certain amenities in their city—the local symphony orchestra or professional sports team, for example—even if they never patronize them. The owners of such establishments cannot, of course, send a bill to everyone who merely appreciates their existence, but they can still earn enough profit to stay in business despite this "failure." It is not necessary to insure that each and every person who enjoys a historic monument pays for it. All that is necessary for that monument's continued existence is that more dollars be collectable from that use of the property than would be from some other use.

There is always the possibility, if there are enough "free riders" anxious to see the monument, but not willing to pay for the privilege, that the monument might be used for advertising purposes. The most obvious way would be to erect billboards on and about the edifice. But this might well detract from its beauty or its historic character. Alternatively, the commercial message could be delivered far away from the structure itself—on the radio, on TV or in print. Hey, perfection is denied us on this side of the Garden of Eden. The market is not perfect in the sense of fully satisfying each and every one of our desires, fully. It is just that all market transactions are mutually beneficial, at least in the ex ante sense, and no other institution can even come close to making this claim; certainly not government, which might be defined as economics at the point of a bayonet.

Under governmental zoning, when property felt to be of historical interest is declared a landmark, it may not be altered, improved, or demolished. Although it is (or was) private property, the owner has been relieved of valuable rights.

Costs, or the alternative uses of the space occupied by the building, are not considered. Sufficient antiquarianism is the only criterion. Unlike antiques on the market, such monuments need not be more valuable as relics than when put to other uses; they need only have *some* worth from a historical perspective in order to be saved.

Thus, there is little likelihood that consumer welfare will be increased by landmark zoning. Instead, a small group of antiquarian elitists can ignore the desires of the rest of the population and impose the preservation of an excessive number of historical buildings.

Perhaps one reason people accept such a policy is that it is difficult to discern the "might-have-beens." The historic landmark is *there*; people see it, enjoy it, photograph it, touch it. It is more difficult to appreciate the factory that might have taken its place, or to envision the extra employment its construction would have meant or the lower-priced consumer goods it could have produced. It is all but impossible to envision the high-rise apartment house that might have occupied that real estate instead, thus pushing rents down.

These possibilities are no less important, however, despite the difficulty of imagining them.

In a case in Berkeley, California, an antiquarian elitist group took action to save an utterly undistinguished small house slated for demolition on the city's blue-collar, industrial west side. It was to have been replaced by a multiunit, multistory apartment building. Then, a neighborhood busybody learned that the single-family house on Fifth Street had been built in 1878, making it one of Berkeley's oldest structures. The antiquarian elitists in the area, who signed the busybody's petition and began agitating to have the current owners of the building deprived of their property rights, have acknowledged that even at its birth, this building would have been plain, quite different from its gingerbread cousins of the period, that it had long since been altered from its original design, and that it was described as blight by some neighbors. Nevertheless, they maintain, pompously, that the rich should not be able to buy and destroy the history of the poor. By attempting to prevent the demolition of the old house, however, they themselves are helping to destroy the future of the poor who might have benefited from the new employment and the new wealth the project would bring to their community.

This issue is also of great relevance to my home town, New Orleans. This city, perhaps, has more historic buildings than any other, at least proportionately to its total. Yes, if these homes were to be demolished, en masse, an important part of the character of the Big Easy would be lost. Tourism, to say the least, would decline. What is at present largely responsible for preventing such an alteration are statist building codes aimed at historical preservation. But, as this chapter demonstrates, this sledge hammer approach constitutes a violation of private property rights; there is no suggestion that this bureaucratic modality will lead to the optimal number of historical buildings; rather, that their number will never change (barring bribes, graft, etc). But, with the private alternatives sketched out above, these externalities can be internalized with the scalpel technique of the marketplace. If all the streets in the French Quarter, for example, were privatized, that would go a long way toward an association comprising all the owners of this area of the city tying each other up with restrictive covenants, ensuring the preservation of heritage buildings. Had this sort of thing been in operation when this real estate was first developed, the problems of the "hold out" would be greatly attenuated.

VII. THE POLITICALLY INCORRECT

26.

THE BAD SAMARITAN

In the Bible, the tale of the Good Samaritan is a dramatic one. After other travelers have passed by the man lying by the side of the road in need of aid, the Good Samaritan alone stops to succor him.

And the moral of the story is clear: if you help the less fortunate, you will be rewarded. In the "modern version" of the account, the Good Samaritan is a social worker who, coming upon a bleeding victim of assault and battery lying in the street, exclaims, "Oh, the poor socially deprived muggers who did this! They must have felt awful to have perpetrated such a foul deed. I must go and comfort them."

So far, there is nothing amiss for the libertarian. The code of non-aggression certainly does not prohibit the provision of aid to our fellow man in need.

But this idyllic scene was rudely interrupted with the enactment of "Good Samaritan" legislation in Minnesota. This law required that witnesses come to the aid of anyone in "grave physical danger," and anyone who fails to do that is subject to misdemeanor charges and a fine of up to $200. The statute did not demand that passers-by undertake acts of heroism by thrusting themselves into violent or potentially violent situations. In such instances only "reasonable assistance" was mandated, such as summoning help from the police.

This initiative was prompted by the New Bedford, Massachusetts, case in which a woman was raped on a pool table in front of several onlookers, and by the famous Kitty Genovese episode, in which a lady was brutally and fatally stabbed on a street in Queens, New York, in the clear sight of dozens of people from their apartment windows in nearby high rise apartment buildings.

According to Minnesota state Rep. Randy Staten, the author of the measure, "Previously, an expert lifeguard could watch a six-month-old baby crawl into the river and drown and sit by or do nothing about it and nothing would happen . . . That is totally unacceptable conduct for a civilized society."

But this will not do. Any lifeguard who sat idly by while a six-month-old baby (or anyone else for that matter) drowned in front of his very eyes, would at the very least be guilty of contract violation. The lifeguard was hired, presumably, to obviate this very occurrence. That he lifted not one finger to prevent it most certainly would have been penalized—long before the passage of the Minnesota Good Samaritan Act.

Of course, if an *off-duty* lifeguard, or any other private citizen not contractually obligated to engage in rescue operations, saw a drowning, he would be under no legal requirement to come to the aid of the victim.

This is the nub of the dispute. According to the Minnesota code, the observer must either rescue the victim or, at the very least, notify the authorities of the problem. But in the libertarian law code, one is bound only to refrain from the commission of aggression. In this philosophy, there are no positive responsibilities incumbent upon the moral agent apart from those he takes upon himself, through contractual agreement.

There is in libertarian circles a debate as to whether or not specific contractually obligated performance can be compelled.

"MINISTER, I'M DELIGHTED TO REPORT THAT
AS A RESULT OF OUR MODERNIZATION PROGRAM,
81% OF OUR WITCH DOCTORS NOW HAVE BEEPERS!"

A promises to sing at B's wedding for a fee; they sign a contract to that effect. At the last minute, A begs off. Certainly, according to one side of this argument, A should forfeit his fee. As well, his reputation will suffer. And, if he posted a performance bond, that, too, would go by the boards. But according to this view, A should not be dragged kicking and screaming to B's wedding and forced under threat of violence to sing. In my view, though, there would be two types of contracts. One would specify that specific performance cannot be compelled, and the other that it can (presumably, the latter would pay more to the performer). If A were to renege, then he legally could be compelled to perform. This makes little sense, as a practical matter for wedding songs, but more for lifeguards at swimming pools. Suppose the following: C hires D to hold a rope for him; if D drops the rope, C will fall to his death. D decides to walk away from this contract and is willing to forfeit his fee. For some reason, only D can hold the rope.

E, C's friend, sees D about to drop the rope and threatens D that if he does so, E will shoot him. Justified? Yes, in my view.

We can perhaps judge between these polar opposite ethical world-views by considering two dimensions: the practical and the logical.

What pragmatic considerations militate against compulsory good Samaritanism? Given that the goal is to promote mutual aid between and amongst the members of our species, is legal coercion the best way, or even a reasonable means toward this end?

There is evidence that weighs in against such a hypothesis. First of all, the Genovese killing and the pool table rape are newsworthy precisely because it is so exceedingly rare for people to stand by and see their fellow creatures hard done by. For every such event there are literally hundreds if not thousands of cases where people pluck little girls out of the paths of onrushing trucks, rescue the elderly from burning buildings, beat the woods for lost children and extricate victims from mine cave-ins, ocean mishaps, etc., often at much expense, at great personal risk, and continued long past the time when the venture can be expected to be met with success. Statistical evidence of this claim—awards for acts of bravery and heroism, for example—is in great abundance.

And certainly none of this activity has been motivated by a fear of running afoul of the law. Heroic deeds of this sort have been taking place since the dawn of recorded history, and the Minnesota enactment was a relatively recent occurrence. More to the point, were this legislation copied elsewhere, and as diligently enforced as its adherents might wish, how many of these heroic rescuers might *refrain* from such activities? Motivations for holding back might include resentment that positive acts are now required by law. But it may also be prompted by a fear to become involved at all, even as a bystander: for the Minnesota law also provided the "victim" with a further avenue of relief, the right to launch a civil lawsuit against the "Bad Samaritan," the person who could come to the rescue, or notify the authorities, but refuses to do so.

Another practical problem is that in many cases of distress (e.g., drowning), an actual rescue is the only response that will be of any help. By the time a witness can inform anyone else of the tragedy, the possibility of effecting aid may be long past. But the Minnesota law specifically exempted from culpability those who seek help from third parties instead of attempting an extrication of the sufferer. Presumably, it would not have been politically feasible to visit punishment on citizens unwilling to risk their own lives in Samaritan ventures. This half way measure, then, falls short of compelling the only act that might be of sufficient help.

Even in the case where mere notification can be of some use (rape, robbery in process) there is a pragmatic difficulty. In order to give warning, the onlookers will often have to travel *away* from the scene of the crime (at least before the era of cell phones). If such a person is really unwilling to perform the required deed, it is easy for him to evade it under such circumstances, and difficult to prove otherwise.

But the impediments to this legislation run far deeper than mere practicality. There are also philosophical dilemmas.

As well, a quandary arises with regard to causal antecedents. In the cases of flood, fire, drowning, violence, etc., it is rather straightforward to identify the reason for the problem, and thus, at least in principle, to effect a rescue. But there are thousands of people who die, and are therefore ready from some form of deliverance for a would-be Good Samaritan, because of antecedents that are unclear, at least to some people.

Consider Ethiopian starvation, a problem much in the news during the years when the Minnesota law was touching off a flurry of Good Samaritan legislation. (We rule out of court that the Ethiopians are foreigners and therefore undeserving of "protection" under the Minnesota Good Samaritan law. For the underlying philosophy of this legislation is the Biblical exhortation that each of us act as if he were "his brother's keeper." Thus this enactment has application not only in one country, but throughout the world.) There are numerous hypotheses that have been attempted to explain this phenomenon: drought, civil war, imperialism, lack of foreign aid, socialism, capitalism, etc.

Suppose that a citizen of Minnesota were hauled into court under a statute similar to the one under discussion—that is, a Good Samaritan law which required not merely notification of the authorities but actual action to alleviate distress. Suppose he was charged under such a statute, either by the forces of law and order or, as provided, by a starving Ethiopian under the civil suit provisions. What kind of defense would be open to the Minnesotan?

He could reply that he had contributed to foreign aid to Ethiopia. But this justification could founder on at least two grounds. First, it might fail because foreign aid, far from being a solution to the problem of starvation, was actually a cause of it. Secondly, it might be unsuccessful in that ground although contributing to foreign aid was indeed the appropriate response, the defendant did not donate sufficient funds.

This leads to the question: How much effort must a Good Samaritan put out in order to save life?

The Minnesota law being discussed here is incomplete in the sense that it left open the question of how much "society," or the "authorities," are to do for the victim. If all that need be done is to notify the government of a needy person, and then the government can sit on its hands and do nothing, then the whole process is null and void.

So we ask again of this "brother's keeper" philosophy: How much must the Good Samaritan do for others?

There are only two responses. All others are merely variants of one or the other. One possibility is that the Good Samaritan weighs the lives of all other people as on a par with his own. In this system, he will continue to give of himself and of his wealth until the problem is solved or his wealth is exhausted. In the Ethiopian case, this result ensues no matter what the cause of the starvation. If the famine there is due to lack of foreign aid (not bloody likely), the Good Samaritan must continue to donate until the problem is solved—or until he is no longer better off than they are. If the starvation is due to the lack of a free market in Ethiopia, the Good Samaritan must likewise keep donating to the cause—only this time it will be the cause of promoting the free enterprise system in Ethiopia—again until either the problem is solved, or his financial circumstances are no better than those of the Ethiopians. For at any less extreme point than this, say, after the Minnesotan has given away virtually all of his treasure, but still has about ten times as much as the Ethiopian, the problem will yet remain: the Ethiopian will still be starving, although perhaps to a lesser or slower degree, and the Minnesotan will still have the wherewithal necessary to save him. (How quickly does the victim need to be dying in order that the Minnesotan will not be considered guilty of violating the Good Samaritan law? We can, perhaps, rule out "dying of old age," but what of cancer? What of cigarette smoking? Will the Minnesotan be guilty if he does not grab the cigarettes out of the hands of any smokers he comes across?)

The only real alternative is the polar opposite to "brother's keeperism": the complete renunciation of the Good Samaritan philosophy, and the embracing of the libertarian alternative of no positive obligation at all.

But we have not yet concluded the case against the Good Samaritan law. What other defense could be made by the Minnesotan charged with its violation? Suppose he claimed he was a research scientist, hurrying to his laboratory to find a cure for cancer, or for AIDS, or for the aging process. Suppose he claimed he engaged in recreation or spent his time in any other way, only in order to most efficiently pursue these ends? (After all, all work and no play, besides making Johnny a dull boy, interferes with the "creative juices.") In either case, in this defense, he would have to concede that one person in trouble would have to make do without the good offices of the researcher. (Could this status as a researcher be self-definitional? Or would one need a Ph.D. in biochemistry from Harvard, or, failing that, from the University of Minnesota? If so, how would we deal with the undoubted fact that numerous and wondrous discoveries have been made in the basement laboratories of "unqualified" *tinkerers*?) But surely, it would be contended, more "Good Samaritan credits" should be garnered by a researcher who saves ten million lives in ten years than by one who helps to save one life today. What, in other words, is the proper discount rate for life saving?

This problem is, of course, as silly as it is intractable. It is impossible to determine any such proper rate of exchange between aiding the troubled in the present and doing so in the future. Any attempted solution to this problem is bound to founder on the question of interpersonal comparison of utilities—the fact that people disagree about what things are valuable and how valuable they are.

Will the defense be allowed to plead ignorance? It is well established that "ignorance of the law is no excuse," but what about ignorance of suffering? In this modern era of TV news, it is exceedingly difficult to be unaware of the anguish that takes place around the world. Famines, avalanches, earthquakes, typhoons, mass murders, all too unfortunately, are the stuff of everyday news. In order to obviate such a defense, however, will the government of Minnesota have to launch a compulsory program of civics and current events education?

The Good Samaritan law adopted in Minnesota was arbitrary and capricious, and it leads down a slippery slope toward massive income redistribution of a kind that may not have been foreseen by its original adherents. The burden of proof would appear to lie with the proponents of any doctrine; yet no proof has as much as been offered for the contention which underlies this statute: the "brother's keeper" argument. It is for all these reasons that the Bad Samaritan, the person who refuses to be stampeded into Good Samaritanism, must be applauded.

27.

THE DUELIST

The common view on dueling is that it is a relic of a bygone era—an uncivilized, primitive, savage, bygone era. All modern, progressive, forward-looking societies now prohibit this practice. And for good reason, it is alleged. For with the duel, the strong would kill off the weak, big bully types would run over everyone else, and the meek would never live long enough to inherit anything at all, let alone the entire Earth.

However, this widely accepted view is nothing but a tissue of fallacies. The critiques of settling matters through combat are without substance; its great benefits have been ignored.

The first thing to be made clear about dueling, though, is that it is an *offer*, not a *threat*. For a duel to take place, *both* parties must agree. In other words, a duel can only take place between consenting adults, and, as such, should command the tolerance that men of good will give to all such actions.

Consider a case in which A says to B, "If you don't voluntarily duel with me, I'm going to kick your ass anyway." Now this statement is clearly a threat. As such, it would be prohibited by the libertarian legal code.

An offer is something you are just as free to accept as to reject; no force, or threat of force, will be applied to you if you reject the offer. Thus, in the case of an offer of a duel, if the invited person refuses to participate, that is the end of the matter. The initiator of the duel cannot persist. If he does, this only shows that the original "offer" was no such thing. Rather, it was really a threat; the "request" was really a demand. As long as it is a bona fide *offer*, a mere refusal is an end to the matter.

If B refuses an "offered" duel, and A uses or threatens violence against him, thus showing up the original "offer" for the threat that it was, A is just as guilty of aggressive behavior in the present system, which outlaws voluntary dueling, as he would be in a system of law that allowed it. We must therefore reject the claim against legalized voluntary dueling that force is involved.

Of course, if you refuse a duel, you may be subjected to all sorts of nonaggressive, nonviolent sanctions. You may be called a coward. Strictly speaking, however, this can in no way violate anyone's rights. Sticks and stones can surely break your bones and violate your rights, but mere name calling can do neither.

It is true, of course, that being called a coward can cause psychological harm, but whether it does so or not is to a very great degree under the control of each individual person. Thanks to the pioneering work of the psychologist Albert Ellis, and his colleague, Dr. Michael Edelstein, author of *Three Minute Therapy*, the ability of the individual to avert harm from coming to himself in situations such as these is becoming more widely recognized.

Dr. Albert Ellis is a twentieth century follower of Epictetus, a philosopher of the first century A.D. At the core of the philosophy of Epictetus is the view that "men are disturbed not by things, but by the views which they take of them." Thus it is that Dr. Ellis holds that psychological harm is caused not so much by being called a coward as by *the view you take of being subjected to such name calling*.

If you take an irrational view of being called a coward, you will harm yourself. If you take a rational view of it, you will not harm yourself. The point that cannot be stressed too strongly is that the choice of which view to take is completely up to you. In other words, it is completely up to the individual to *choose* whether or not to be psychologically harmed by being called a coward.

An irrational view would be the following: "Oh horrors, it's *awful* to be called a coward. This shouldn't be. It's unfair. *I can't stand this.* I'll never be able to face people. They'll hate me. They'll despise me. And that will be even more awful, even more intolerable. I'll have to keep hidden. But how will I even be able to face myself? I'll have to commit suicide." Thinking thoughts such as these will lead straight to psychological harm.

On the other hand, one could choose to take a more sane approach. One could choose to say something like: "It is true that I will have to pay a penalty for refusing to duel. When the duelist calls me a coward for refusing to fight him, there will be several people who will refuse to have anything further to do with me. This is unfortunate, regrettable, and a pain in the ass. But life is full of just such occurrences. And even though I won't like it, *I will be able to stand it.* Actually, I could tolerate much worse, should it come to that. Limiting though these penalties may be, I have judged in a calm, rational mood, that it would be still *worse* to risk death by engaging in combat. So I'll accept the penalties attached to refusing to do so. I won't like them, but I'll make the best of them."

It is, of course, true that it is no small task to be able to really mean it, when one takes the rational approach to a thing like this. It is all too easy to merely mouth the rational words. And this is what Dr. Ellis' "Rational-Emotive-Behavior" therapy is all about: through much practice and a sort of Socratic dialogue with the therapist, really internalizing the rational view, and then learning how to apply it to all sorts of situations. This lesson is so straightforward, that Ellis' colleague, Dr. Michael Edelstein, has demonstrated that it can be done in "three minutes."

Dueling is a legitimate activity that should be legalized; the *offer* of a duel cannot hurt anyone (except possibly in a psychological way); the *demand* for a duel should be illegal, just as it now is.

Now consider the vantage point of the masochist. All too often, the rights of the masochist are completely ignored; the case of dueling is no exception. As the law stands now, with dueling prohibited, the masochist is completely stripped of his right to engage in a duel. It is, of course, true that the motivation of a masochist for entering a duel is virtually the opposite of the motivation most people would have for doing such a thing. Instead of aiming to wound or kill his antagonist, the masochist aims to be himself injured. This should make no difference, however, as far as the rights and wrongs of the case are concerned. If we but grant the right of suicide to the masochist—and it is hard to see how any libertarian could refuse to do so—then his right to be killed in a duel would seem to follow logically. The right to commit suicide, it will be remembered, follows directly from the self ownership we each have in our own persons. Once the right of self ownership is granted, suicide and dueling follow directly. The masochist should have the right of any adult to do anything whatever, provided mutual consent is involved, and provided the action concerns only those consenting adults involved in it.

A possible criticism of this case is based on questioning the claim that any such masochistic action necessarily concerns "only one person." Suppose, it is argued, that the masochist who duels is a husband and father who has a wife and children dependent upon him. In this case, would it not be illegitimate for the masochist to duel? And since almost everyone has *someone* at least partially dependent upon him for support, then it would follow that it is wrong for almost everyone to duel (or otherwise unnecessarily to risk his life). Therefore, the prohibition can be justified.

There are several things wrong with this criticism. First of all, it flies in the face of the doctrine of self ownership. If a

person *may not* risk his life legally because there are people dependent upon him, then to that extent he is not free. But if he is not, then those who are dependent upon him are his owners, or slave masters, since they control him. So this criticism of dueling amounts to the advocacy of slavery.

Moreover, if the family is dependent upon the breadwinner, he is also dependent upon them. (How else can we explain his frequent willingness to abide by their decisions as to what vocations he should enter and what risks he should take?) But if he is dependent upon them, then for the same reasons that he has to follow their orders about risky behavior, *they* have to follow *his* views on risky behavior. In other words, if he can be construed as a slave of theirs, then they can with equal logic (or lack of logic) be construed as slaves of his.

And if they are truly slaves of his, then he can order them to allow him to do any risky thing they fear. They must obey his order that they allow him to duel; otherwise they would be disobedient slaves, and that would never do. But by the same token, they can order him not to give them the order to allow him to duel. And so on. The point here is that it is an entirely illogical situation for one person to be both a slave and an owner of another person—the *same* other person. And this illogic is logically derivable from the criticism of voluntary dueling on the ground that a potential duelist has "responsibilities."

What of the choice of weapons? Presumably, this should lie with the person challenged, not with the challenger. Traditionally, this was always the case. However, it was typically limited to swords, fisticuffs or pistols. There is no justification for this, however, none at all. Rather, this decision should be broadened; and when I say broadened, I mean just that. Consider now the case of A, who is a crack shot, a mean man with a sword and a boxing champ; he stands at 6'8" and weighs 250 pounds, not an ounce of it fat. He challenges B who is the proverbial 90-pound weakling. B wears glasses as thick as the bottom of Coke bottles, and can hardly see through them. At pistols, he would be more of a danger to himself than anyone else. Swords? B can hardly lift one, let alone *fight* with it. However, he is a chess grandmaster, a world champion at tiddlywinks and a graceful ballerina to boot. It would have to be a particularly brave A who would challenge any such B, given that the latter could choose the skill in which *he* is expert. The point is, everyone is better than someone else at *something*. If this doesn't put the kibosh on *most* dueling, then nothing will. In my own case, I am a *champion* whiner. Let anyone challenge *me* to a duel, and he is a gonner.

28.

THE EXECUTIONER

To some people it might be look like a grotesque joke to consider the hangman in an even slightly positive role, let alone as a heroic figure. This is because the executioner plays a central part in the imposition of the death penalty, and this type of punishment is anathema to many of those who judge human action against a code of ethics. In this view, it is wrong for one man to murder another; nevertheless, it is an act of brutal savagery to then cold-bloodedly kill the murderer. Killing is *always* unjustified in this perspective, and thus two wrongs do not make a right.

In order to show the error of this way of looking at the matter, it will therefore be necessary to justify the ultimate chastisement on moral grounds. In what is to follow, I shall attempt to do just that. But I shall offer a "weak" justification for the death penalty, not a "strong" one. That is, I shall attempt to prove that there are at least *some* cases in which it is ethically appropriate to take the life of a person judged guilty of murder, not that this is always true.

In doing so, I shall have to assume away several objections. First, I stipulate that the convicted murderer is really guilty of committing the crime, and that there were no extenuating circumstances (e.g., self defense) to mitigate the enormity of the act. Secondly, I will not question the jurisdiction of those who would enforce the capital punishment; I assume that this would be done by the "forces of law and order," whoever they are, and that they are entirely innocent of any other wrongdoing, apart perhaps, from undertaking the act in question. Thirdly, I assume there will be no moral damages to the punishers: i.e., that they will not become brutalized and commit crimes on their own account as a result of putting the guilty to death.

Having set the stage in this manner, we are now presented with a murderer and his dead victim. Suppose that there were a machine in existence like the one depicted in the 1990s TV series *Babylon 5*. And this machine had room for two bodies and a switch, which, when activated, could transfer the life out of one body and into the other. That is to say, the live murderer could be dragged, kicking and screaming if need be, into this machine, and placed alongside the murder victim. (The "invention" of this machine was inspired by *Anarchy, State, and Utopia*, author Robert Nozick.)

The ethical question this machine poses for us is this: Would it be just to flick the switch, thereby transferring life from the murderer to the victim? Granted, we do not have access to such a wondrous machine as yet. But given the advances in computing, artificial intelligence, genetic engineering, etc., it is probably only a matter of time before such a machine exists.

To ask the question of whether its use is morally justified is to answer the question. Consider the implications of a negative reply. This would mean that, even though the murderer in effect stole a life from his victim, he shall not be forced to give one back. Can any more unjustified act be imagined? Hardly. Nor can it be considered gratuitous, "cruel and unusual," or unbridled savagery to force the murderer to take part in this somewhat grisly procedure. For in this case, the murderer will not be killed for "no reason at all," which is the way opponents of capital punishment describe what they see as a lust for revenge. On the contrary, he shall be killed so that another, *his innocent victim*, may live. Those who would argue against forcing the murderer to enter the machine are, in effect, advocating that the murderer's life be considered more precious than that of the victim.

It is crucially important that this point be driven home. For it is our only weapon against those who object to capital punishment on moral grounds. By the use of this fanciful machine, we have introduced the cloven foot of capital punishment into the hitherto impregnable fortress built by the opponents of this penalty. We have established that, *for at least one case*, there is justification galore for taking the life of the murderer. What this means is that the lives of *all* murderers are morally forfeit, given the validity of the assumptions we are still making (no possibility of mistakes, no extenuating circumstances, etc.).

We must now relax these artificial assumptions and move back into the real world. We have still established that the murderer's life is morally forfeit. He no longer has a claim over it that must be recognized. Who, then, has a valid title to his life? Since the victim is no longer with us, and cannot be brought back to the land of the living, his heirs are assigned all his worldly possessions. But one of his (un)worldly possessions, as we have seen, is the right to his murderer's very life. True, in the absence of our machine, the victim cannot exercise this right, but he still *has* it, nonetheless. This right then passes on to his heirs, along with all his other rights, property and assigns.

Suppose that the heirs of the victim are a wife and small children. Then the wife becomes the owner of the murderer's life. She alone may properly dispose of it. She may, if she wishes, order that he be killed. Alternatively, she may be a pacifist and agree to forgive him for murdering her husband. However, the victim may have left a will, stipulating, among other things, how he wishes his murderer to be treated, should that occurrence ever take place. If so, then *his* wishes must be respected, not those of his heirs. For their ownership of the life of the murderer is only based on the victim's, which is thus primary. Another option would be for her to allow him to buy his freedom from her. If they can arrive at a mutually agreeable financial settlement, the murderer may be able to get off scot-free. (The murderer and/or his friends and business associates may wish to place the heirs of the victim in an untenable situation by making threats of further aggression. In order to preclude such a situation, a binding pre-arrangement may be arranged with the forces of law and order, which presumably are strong enough to be impervious to such threats.) Last but not least, the widow may insist that the murderer be incarcerated for life at hard labor, the proceeds from which would be used to house and feed herself and her children. There is little doubt that the proceeds from such an arrangement would be positive. Slavery, after all, was an economically viable system, and would have been more so, had there been no serious moral objections to it, as there would not be to the system now being advocated. Then, too, chain gangs were economically practicable. In the modern era, murderers receive three square meals a day, are housed in a warm, dry cell, have TV privileges and medical attention, etc., and, to add insult to injury, the victim's heirs are forced to pay for all this through taxes. Can anything less justified than this be imagined?

Now let us relax the assumption of certainty. In other words, I shall hereby posit the real world situation in this regard. Here, except in such cases as the shooting of Lee Harvey Oswald by Jack Ruby, which was witnessed by scores of people in person, and millions more through the intermediation of television, the facts of any murder can only be known with a greater or lesser degree of probability. And let us further suppose that in one particular case not only was the wrong man accused, seized, tried, convicted, and then executed, but it was later found out, *for sure*, that this tragic mistake had been made. This is surely

214

an occurrence that opponents of the death penalty greatly fear and cite in defense of their position.

By applying our principles once again, no matter how counter-intuitive such a procedure may appear at first sight, we may successfully address this problem. Murder is the unjustified killing of an innocent person. The judge and jury that sentence an innocent man to death, along with the hangman who carries out this penalty, are acting in a manner so as to kill such a person. They are therefore guilty of nothing less than murder! As such, it is *they* who must now be made to pay for their crime. And, there would be no doubt that they had carried out this unjustified execution.

Such a scenario is utterly unrealistic in modern society, of course. But this is because our political leaders fail to consistently apply the law that those who engage in wrongful killing are themselves guilty of criminal behavior. They make an exception for judges, juries, hangmen, etc., who operate according to law, are disinterested and are motivated only by a desire to punish the guilty. But wrongful killing is wrongful killing, no matter whether it is considered legal or not. (I need do no more than cite the findings of the Nuremberg Trials to support this contention), and despite the motivation(s) of the perpetrator(s). Such considerations may help us to distinguish between different *degrees* of guilt—first-degree murder, second-degree murder, manslaughter, etc.—but cannot entirely exculpate blameworthiness.) Further, wrongful killing is murder, which should, in justice, be punishable.

However unlikely, let us just suppose for a moment that this insight were incorporated into the procedures of the legal system. It is not difficult to anticipate that under such a regime judges and juries would be most cautious in their impositions of the death penalty (and to a lesser degree, of course, to impose all other penalties), and hangmen would feel a greater reluctance to ply their trade indiscriminately. The "hanging judge" might still be popular in fictional accounts of justice, but he would not last too long in real life. Thus, even if the death penalty were legalized, there would be no unseemly haste under these conditions to send accused murderers to their final destinations. The bloodbaths feared by death penalty opponents would likely not materialize.

But there is yet one more arrow in the quiver of the advocates of life imprisonment as a maximum penalty. In their view, however justified the activities of the hangman, the death penalty does not decrease the murder rate—its ostensible purpose. In other words, balked in their principled opposition, they now take refuge in mere utilitarian arguments.

But they face difficulties here, too. First of all, a reduction in the murder rate is only one justification for the death penalty. The other, as we have seen, is a matter of principle: only in this way can the life of the victim (possibly) be returned to him. Secondly, the evidence cited by the opponents of the death penalty in support of their utilitarian argument is faulty. It consists mainly of studies which correlate presence or absence of the death penalty with the murder rate (trying to hold constant extraneous factors such as population size, density, wealth variability, poverty level, etc.). And lo and behold, there *is* precious little statistical relation between these two variables.

But Isaac Ehrlich, a more careful investigator, rejected this whole methodology. He reasoned that it was not really presence or absence of the death penalty that would serve as the prime incentive for or against engaging in murder, but rather the rate of executions actually carried out. A given state might retain the ultimate punishment on its books, but if it never acted upon it, this legislation would become a dead letter law, relatively ineffective in changing behavior. Instead of attempting to find a relationship between the law and the number of murders that took place, Ehrlich explored the correlation between the execution and the murder rates. And his evidence is highly revealing. Murderers, just like the rest of us, tend to be rational, and thus influenced by the strength of the penalties imposed upon them.

Nor is it difficult to comprehend the common sense behind Ehrlich's findings. We know that the higher the penalty (given that the probability of its being imposed remains constant), the more likely it is that the proscribed behavior will be deterred. A fifteen-year sentence is more of a threat than incarceration for a decade, and life imprisonment is a sterner penalty than jailing for fifteen years. But the death penalty is surely a far more rigorous punishment than even prison for life. How else to explain the frantic attempt of prisoners on "death row" to put off or rescind entirely their appointment with the electric chair, so that they can "be free" to serve out a life sentence?

Now consider what must go through the mind of a criminal who has just engaged in a particularly heinous act which falls just short of actual murder. With a death penalty law that is actively enforced, the perpetrator is likely to reason as follows: "If I kill my victim, I gain by eliminating a witness who can later testify against me; on the other hand, I risk a far greater penalty if I am caught." Without the death penalty, the likely reasoning is very different. The assessment of the benefits of murder remains as before, but now there is no greater penalty to be set against it. Under these conditions, it is chillingly easy to see why the incidence of murder would rise.

The case in favor of the death penalty, and hence the employment of the executioner, is buttressed by both principled and utilitarian arguments.

A necessary but not sufficient condition for justified punishment in cases of theft is that the perpetrator be made to return what is stolen. Justice could hardly be said to have been done if the thief is allowed to keep his ill-gotten gains while the victim is forced to stand idly by and watch him the thief enjoy his property. If I steal a tooth from you, then, at the very least, justice demands that I be made to give one back to you. This is how the biblical injunction "a tooth for a tooth" may be justified.

But this does not go far enough by half (as it turns out, "by half" is both literally and figuratively correct). Suppose that A steals $100 from B. If justice consists solely of forcing A to give back the $100 to B, it cannot be said that any punishment whatsoever has taken place. A is no worse off than before; however else this return may be described, it cannot be called punishment. At the very least, A should be made to give back B's $100 to him, and then his punishment should consist of doing to A what he had previously done to B, that is, taking $100 from A, this time, and giving it to B. Since transferring $100 from A to B twice over is equivalent to transferring $200 from one to the other, this accounts for the aphorism "two teeth for a tooth." (See Murray N. Rothbard, *The Ethics of Liberty*, Atlantic Highlands, N.J.: Humanities Press, 1982.)

Given the law of "two teeth for a tooth," it is unfortunate that full justice cannot be done, even with the advent of our magical machine. For the murderer really owes his victim not one, but two lives, and our apparatus can only force him to disgorge one of these. If, however, people were like the proverbial cats, and had not one but nine lives, then it is clear that justice could only be accomplished by forcing the murderer into the machine *twice*. This, of course, would allow the victim to stockpile an extra life, for a total of ten.

29.

DWARF THROWER

Dwarves, or little people as they are sometimes called, engage in a variety of professions. But some heed a rather unique calling, that of the use of themselves as human projectiles. Sometimes they are thrown, and the contest depends upon distance, or hang times, or grace through the air, or some other such criterion. On other occasions, they are used as human bowling balls, with the number of pins knocked down as the earmark of success. But, whatever wacky activity they are engaged in, all have two things in common. First, not even one of these midgets is ever forced to take part in these "sports" against his will and only adults can take on these jobs. If any little people were coerced into such occupations, libertarians would be opposed, but to the compulsion, not to the job. Secondly, this practice is universally reviled by all busybodies and do-gooders. In other words, these games consist of "capitalist acts between consenting adults." Thus, they are grist for the mill of this book, which defends behavior which is out of favor on the part of many, and yet violates no stricture of libertarian law.

Why do the little people allow themselves to be used in such a manner? This is similar to the question put to Willie

219

Sutton: "Why do you rob banks?" His answer? "That's where the money is." In like manner, one of the motivating forces in the present context is the lure of the payoff. The practice of dwarf throwing offers more money than many other careers or pastimes.

And what explains that phenomenon? This is part and parcel of the economics of compensating differentials. First, it is a dangerous occupation. They may fly through the air with the greatest of ease, but they must come back down to earth at some point and when they do it is, at the very least, a jarring experience, no matter how much padding they wear. Secondly, many of these diminutive human beings may well have an aversion to being treated in such a manner. If so, it will take even more in the way of compensation to induce them to put up with what they regard, quite reasonably, as an indignity. If these are not their motivations, wages will be unaffected. If they enjoy the experience and see the social aspects of their calling in a positive manner, then money wages will fall as they queue up to take these jobs.

Economists know that, all things considered, dwarves make a profit on every "jump" they undergo. Were this not the case, they would scarcely agree to be used in such a manner. If a dwarf is paid one hundred dollars to be hurled, we can deduce that all the negative aspects of this experience—the risk of being injured, the alternatives they must forego to take part in this game, the possible shame they may suffer—are together of less import to them than the amount of money they are paid. The difference is profit accruing to the midget.

Why do the do-gooders do what they do? Why are they dead set in their attempt to call a halt to these goings on? Part of the explanation must be that they are would-be dictators, ever ready to impose their views over the choices made by others. Another part may be that they are disgusted by the specter of people being (mis)treated in this manner. Further, they may be poor economists and do not realize that *all* voluntary acts are necessarily beneficial at least in the ex ante sense. That is, after being tossed the small person may come to regret what he has done (or, rather, allowed to be done to him). For example, he may wish he had not participated in the tossing if he is injured, or "outed" to his family. But, beforehand, he *expected* more benefit than harm, or he would not have agreed to the deal.

However, the same may be said of *any* human action from buying, selling, renting, gambling, indeed, getting out of bed in the morning. We all engage in such acts because we perceive the gain as greater than the loss. And, as with any activity, sometimes we err. Thus there is nothing unique about dwarf tossing.

Then, too, the same considerations apply to the manager who organizes dwarf bowling. He, too, expects to make a profit: the returns from the ticket sales will be greater than all the costs. Sometimes, he also can be disappointed.

So, no matter how reviled is this practice, it is one that must be permitted in the free society. And, for agreeing to be thrown, in the face of ridicule, opprobrium, and revulsion, the dwarf tossee (and tosser as well) must be considered heroic.

30.

INTELLECTUAL-PROPERTY DENIER

Most people hold the view that just as we can legitimately own pencils, puppies, and pickles, it is proper for us to attain property rights in our ideas. After all, our thoughts emanate from inside us, from the very core of our being. It would be unjust if we could not own what we produce in this way. Certainly, our laws are now predicated on this perspective. As well, there is a utilitarian aspect of this argument: unless intellectual property is protected by law, it is contended, research and development in new ideas will atrophy and the progress of mankind will come to an abrupt halt.

There are two main protections of intellectual property (IP). In the case of patents, a new invention must be registered with the authorities, and the first inventor to do so has the right to sell or keep for his own use the entire benefits of his breakthrough for a given number of years. There are two problems with this scenario, both of them fatal to the argument. First, what about the independent inventor? A and B have both worked for years to create their identical invention. A gets to the patent office five minutes before B. A has 100% ownership over this new innovation, while B gets absolutely nothing. This state of affairs is entirely incompatible with the justification for IP in the first place: that everyone should be able to own the fruits of their own creativity. Well, what about poor B? Shouldn't he also get to own this invention, without having to pay A any licensing fee? (We stipulate here that B was indeed an independent inventor and learned nothing from A's efforts.)

The second flaw in the argument for patents is the time limit on ownership. With regard to my pencils, puppies, and pickles, I own them permanently, not merely for some arbitrary amount of time. Not only do I own them for as long as I want, I can give them to my heirs. If I really own my ideas as advocates of IP claim, then, I should own them forever. But this creates insuperable performative contradiction problems for that viewpoint. For, if we can all own ideas, then we can all have private property in words, given that words are merely one manifestation of ideas. In the last sentence, I used 25 words. There were 5 repeats: "can," "all," "we," "words", "ideas." This gives a total of 20 words that I utilized. But, each of these words was originally *created* by someone else. For example, the word "for," we may suppose, was first thought of by Mr. For; the word "if" by Mr. If, the word "we," by Mr. We, etc. If IP were justified, it would be improper of me to use any of these 20 words without permission of their *owners*. No such permission has ever been forthcoming to me, nor to anyone else. But our problems do not end here. For each and every word in the English language was created by *someone*. And this does not apply merely to that one language. Rather, it transcends them all. Thus, if IP were correct, none of us could use *any* words. We could not speak and we could not write. We could not even grunt, since Mr. Grunt started that one up. This pertains, too, to the person who defends IP. Based on his own philosophy, he could not licitly articulate his viewpoint; for to do so would require words, and he is forbidden on the basis of his own philosophy to use any extant words. He could make up new ones, such as zxcvcxv, poiuwerkjls and lkjmwmkls, but it would be rather difficult to communicate anything in this manner, let alone defend IP. As for those of us who do not accept this perspective, we are entirely free to counter IP with the use of words. (I owe this idea of the performative contradiction to Hans Hoppe.)

It will be objected that I am carrying things too far. Hey, that's the entire point of the *reductio ad absurdum* argument: to take claims seriously and to their logical conclusion. Sometimes, it is easier to see the fallacy of an argument when it is writ large in this manner. The advocate of IP has no right to say that it applies only for a certain number of years and/or not to language. If ideas should really be owned by their creators, then there is no possible logical objection to analyzing what this really means, as we have just done. It logically implies that the advocates of this view maintain silence.

The second protection for IP is copyright. This, too, is time denominated. Typically, copyrights last for some number of years, sometimes a half century after the demise of the author. Again, we note this cannot be made compatible with ownership property, which has no time limitation.

But copyrights have a better deontological (rights oriented or ethical) status than patents. There is no question of one creator receiving 100% of the benefits, and another, who also deserves credit for the innovation (based on the IP philosophy), coming away with none. Then, too, copyright benefits from being contractually based, something also missing from the patent arena.

Still, these two different means of creating property rights in ideas suffer from the same difficulty: the entire purpose of property rights is to reduce, nay, eliminate conflicts over scarce goods. If ownership over goods and services is fully specified and all are law-abiding, then no conflict can arise. But, no conflict need ever arise with ideas because once known, *all* parties can use them. The utilization of an idea by one person does not in the least detract from the use of that same idea by another or others. Suppose girl A is the first to put her hair up into a ponytail. Girl B sees this and arranges her own hair in the same style. Did B steal anything from A? No. B's ponytail in no way detracts from A's hairstyle. It is not as if B went over to A and ruined or erased her hairdo. A's ponytail is undisturbed when B makes use of this idea. We can have our cake, here, and eat it too. My use of the Pythagorean Theorem in no way detracts from your use of it. To create property rights in ideas, then, is to substitute scarcity where no scarcity need exist. Scarcity is the enemy of well-being. A successful economy reduces scarcity, not increases it.

But what about copyright contracts? X creates a book or a song or a new machine or a formula for a drug. He sells it to Y, not outright, but with one proviso: that Y not copy it without X's permission (for which X will charge Y). X is, in effect, selling Y the right to use this new innovation, but not to allow any third party, Z, to avail himself of it. So far, so good. But, Y loses the product and Z finds it. Or Z sees Y (or X) using it and, on the basis of that observation, copies it for his own use or to sell to still others. Has Y violated his contract with X? No. Y is only obligated to not copy what he has purchased, and he did not. Y never contractually agreed to not lose it or shield his use of it from others, such as Z. Did Z engage in any illicit behavior? Certainly he did nothing he was contractually obliged to refrain from, since it was Y, not Z, who agreed not to copy.

Let us now move from deontological considerations to utilitarian ones. Now we are concerned not with the rights of the matter, but with which system will create more wealth. At first glance, it would appear that this consideration is all on the side of IP. After all, goes the usual refrain, if inventors, artists, and creators cannot retain ownership of their own ideas they will have less or no incentive to create them in the first place. Without IP, intellectual creativity, innovation, research, invention, etc., would wither and perhaps die.

True, without this added incentive, assuming all other things equal, there would be less of this sort of activity.

However, other things are decidedly not equal. Once patents are granted (and/or copyrights become the order of the day), these serve as barriers to follow up on new innovation. Yes, when the very first patents were granted, this phenomenon did not exist. But as IP piles up, new breakthroughs become harder and more difficult to come by. For now, the inventor must keep his eye not only on what he himself is trying to accomplish, but also on other IP rights, so as to not transgress upon them. That is, extant IP serves as a sort of obstacle course against the development of new knowledge. IP has also given rise to numerous lawsuits over patents and copyrights. Thus, thousands of technical people, engineers, scientists, who could have been engaged in the process of research and development, instead make it their profession to serve as expert witnesses for plaintiffs and/or defendants in IP cases.

Also interfering with the unearthing of scientific knowledge is a practice known as "submarining." Here, a high-tech firm applies for a patent, but does not disclose it to the public. It then uses a continuation, so as to later reapply for this patent. Its strategy is to await further developments in this field and then reapply after others have filled in the gaps. It can take advantage of its earlier application date to, in effect, prevent latecomers from benefiting from their own research.

So, does IP, on balance, lead to more or less scientific break-through? It is difficult to say. This is an empirical question and the correct answer may change from time to time. That is, in some years, more ideas will be created as a result of IP, and in others, fewer. As we have seen, there are opposing forces that result from IP, some tending in the direction of more idea creation, others not.

What is the optimal amount of research and development? From the utilitarian point of view, it sounds as if we can never have enough of it, but, surely, that is mistaken. For if it took up anything like a majority of our income, we would die for lack of food, shelter, medical care, etc. In order to maximize

"TELL HIM THAT THROUGH A GENEALOGICAL SEARCH, HE HAS BEEN FOUND TO BE A DESCENDANT OF THE GREEK POET AND DRAMATIST AESCHYLUS WHO LIVED FROM 525 TO 456 B.C., AND UNDER THE LIBRARY COMPENSATION FUND FOR AUTHORS, WE HAVE A CHECK FOR HIM FOR $8.18"

expected wealth, resources should be allocated in such a manner so that no more income can be attained by switching a marginal dollar's worth from one activity to another. Given that we cannot determine with any reasonable confidence whether IP will enhance this process or retard it, the ideal resource allocation is the one compatible with libertarian law.

There were two elements we must address: the deontological, and the pragmatic (how much research will be done in the absence of IP "rights?") For the libertarian, the first is crucial; the correct or optimal amount of R&D is precisely the amount that would be done if the law were just, that is, entirely without IP. So, even if zero R&D occurred under this system, that would be the proper amount.

Consider now this objection: "But what about something that has no live performance equivalent?" First, I don't think there is any such thing. Suppose I make a great movie or game and receive zero revenue from my efforts in creating it, not even the amount I will get from having the time advantage of being first (e.g., the examples of paperback vs. hardcover books; theater movies vs. DVDs, Paris dresses vs. Macy's knock-offs). Well, movies and games will still be produced, only not, directly, for money. What other benefits to me might there be? There are conferences of devotees of movies and games. My speaking fees at them will be elevated. I can get an endowed chair at a university in their film department. Microsoft, IBM, and Google will start a bidding war for my services. Then, there is benevolence. I might win an Oscar award for best movie. Does that pay money? I'm not sure. Even if not, I'll still be a popular boy. Groupies will shower their favors on me, etc.

To conclude: There is no property rights violation if a company invests millions creating a piece of game software or a movie, and technology tricks allow any consumer to copy the end product at zero cost (to the consumer). This very extreme example only means that people will still make movies or games, but not based on the profit motivation.

INDEX

231

Terra Libertas Publishing House
www.terralibertas.com

The Tragedy of the Euro
Philipp Bagus

The Law
Frédéric Bastiat

That Which is Seen, and That Which is Not Seen
Frédéric Bastiat

Economic Sophisms
Frédéric Bastiat

Harmonies of Political Economy
Frédéric Bastiat

Defending the Undefendable
Walter Block

Building Blocks for Liberty
Walter Block

Principles of Economics
Carl Menger